THE POWYS JOURNAL

Volume XX

THE POWYS SOCIETY

The Powys Society is a registered charity, No 801332.

The Powys Society was founded in 1967 to 'establish the true literary status of the Powys family through promotion of the reading and discussion of their works', in particular those of John Cowper Powys (1872–1963), Theodore Francis Powys (1875–1953), and Llewelyn Powys (1884–1939).

The Society publishes a journal and three newsletters a year, and has an active publication programme. In addition it organises an annual weekend conference, occasional meetings, exhibitions, and walks in areas associated with the Powys family.

The Society is an international one, attracting scholars and non-academics from around the world, and welcomes everyone interested in learning more about this remarkable family.

Correspondence and membership enquiries should be addressed to the Hon. Secretary

Chris Thomas

Flat D, 87 Ledbury Road, London W11 2AG
(tel: 020 7243 0168)

Visit the Powys Society Web Site:
www.powys-society.org

THE POWYS JOURNAL

Volume XX

2010

Editor
Richard Maxwell

Contributing Editor
Charles Lock

The Powys Journal is a publication of The Powys Society, appearing annually each summer. Its aim is to publish original material by the Powys family—in particular, John Cowper Powys, Theodore Francis Powys and Llewelyn Powys—and scholarly articles and other material relating to them and their circle. It also carries reviews of books by and about the Powys family and their circle.

The Powys Journal is grateful to the copyright holders of the individual estates and their literary agents for their permission to print or to quote from the writings of John Cowper Powys, Theodore Francis Powys and Llewelyn Powys.

MSS **for publication and correspondence** about the contents of the *Journal* should be addressed to the Editor, **Charles Lock**, Professor of English Literature, University of Copenhagen, Njalsgade 130, DK–2300 Copenhagen S, Denmark; his e-mail address is:

lock@hum.ku.dk

The Powys Journal has a refereeing policy, whereby material is submitted for independent assessment. In order that the anonymity of the author and referee is preserved, articles should omit the name of the author. Please send submissions if possible by e-mail: they can be in text-only format or RTF or in Microsoft Word, but not any other word-processing programme, and should have the minimum of formatting.

Authors of printed articles will receive two copies of the *Journal*.

Orders for copies of the *Journal* should be addressed to the Society's Hon. Secretary, whose address is shown on page 2.

Cover and title-page design: Bev Craven

Typeset in Adobe Caslon
in PageMaker 6.5 on a Macintosh computer
by Stephen Powys Marks

Printed and bound by Hobbs the Printers Ltd, Totton, Hampshire

ISSN 0962–7057

ISBN 978–1–874559–40–5

CONTENTS

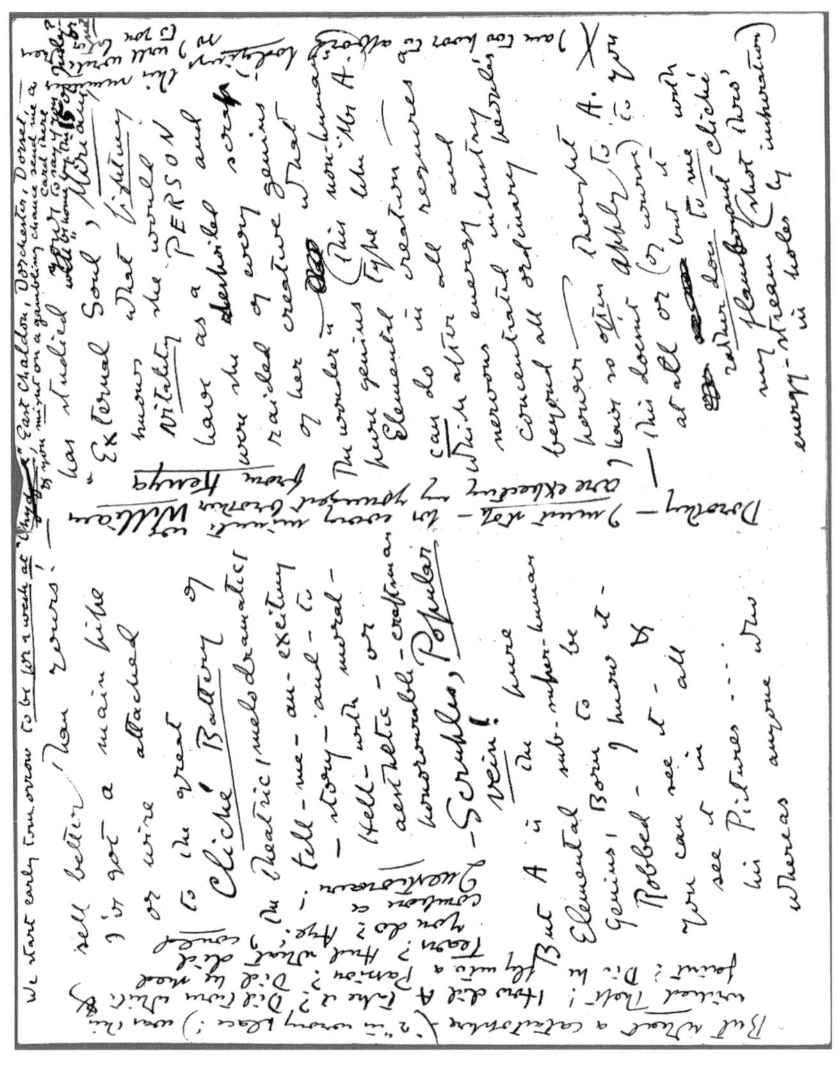

Part of letter from John Cowper Powys to Dorothy M. Richardson 7 July 1938. (Beinecke Library, Yale University)

All editing involves a compromise between the vivacity of script and the clarity of print, and this photograph shows how much is lost of the character and expressiveness of JCP's script when a letter is printed; it also shows how much can be gained by those wishing to read the letter in an orderly sequence without 'graphic distractions'. See Review on page 168. Thanks to Max Peltier for the scan.

EDITORIAL

John Cowper Powys could be remarkably discerning in his literary judgements. This has been somewhat obscured by the gushings of praise disbursed in correspondence with younger writers whose names are hardly known today except as recipients of letters from John Cowper. In the late 1930s Powys was, in a good-humoured way, reproached by Emma Goldman for his unrestrained endorsement of her cause, anarchism: 'If I thought you an Irishman, I should suspect you of having kissed the Blarney Stone, you say so many nice and flattering things. Still, I am grateful ....' Yet when there were no personal obligations in the way, John Cowper's views could be uncannily far-reaching, as in the letter to Louis Wilkinson of 29 September 1948: 'The best to my mind of modern American writers is a certain Saul Bellow who has only written 2 books'. Earlier, in the 1920s, John Cowper's recognition of Dorothy M. Richardson makes for the most incisive link between Powys and modernist writing in Britain. While there's no record of Powys ever communicating with Bellow, his correspondence with Richardson, edited by Janet Fouli and published by Cecil Woolf in 2008, must be counted the most significant appearance of John Cowper's letters since those to his brother Llewelyn, some thirty years ago. John Cowper usually wrote to younger writers because they had written in admiration to him; with Dorothy Richardson it was out of admiration for her work that John Cowper initiated the correspondence.

The impact is registered in this issue of *The Powys Journal*: the correspondence is reviewed here at length by Jeff Bursey, while the volume's editor, Janet Fouli, contributes a substantial and revealing essay on 'Reading Women': that is, both the women writers that Powys read, and the women who read Powys. There we learn that though Dorothy M. Richardson was less well known in the United States than in Britain, Phyllis Playter had read and admired the early volumes of *Pilgrimage* before she met John Cowper in 1922. Powys would in 1930 write the first monograph ever published on Dorothy M. Richardson. Until now that short book has been an isolated phenomenon that has received very little attention; eighty years on, we have the means with which to explore this friendship between two of the greatest novelists of the twentieth century. One always feels the tendentiousness of a campaigner in making that claim for John Cowper; to be claiming as much for Richardson should be felt in Powysian circles at least as innocent of partiality. After a life-time reading Powys I have acquired some sense of what others might find unsympathetic or exasperating, even in the great novels. Yet a somewhat less intensive reading of Dorothy M. Richardson over many years has yielded no clue as to why she is not honoured at least as highly as Virginia Woolf. In the history of women's writing over the past hundred years, and in any account of modernism in literature, it is baffling that Richardson should occupy any but a central place. On the evidence of this issue of the *Journal*, Richardson has already (or at last) become a salient presence in the study of John Cowper Powys.

Reading women is a phrase that might be matched by writing women. This volume of *The Powys Journal* contains more contributions by women than by men. Given that John Cowper's attitude to women is neither fashionable nor beyond reproach—Frances Gregg dared to say as much—it is good that these matters are being debated by women readers and scholars. *The Powys Journal* is dedicated to the promotion of the study of all members of the Powys family and their circle; it has become customary for the Editor to observe that this does not mean only the three 'writing brothers' — John Cowper, Theodore Francis and Llewelyn—and to regret that there is very seldom a balanced representation of Powyses in any issue of the *Journal*. The present volume seems to be particularly weighted towards John Cowper. Let it be said (yet again) that submissions are encouraged not only on other members of the family but on their friends, their circles, and indeed on broader contexts, both historical and contemporary. Florence Marie-Laverrou draws our attention to the little-studied *After My Fashion*, and explores the role of Isadora Duncan not so much biographically as a friend of John Cowper's, but in larger cultural terms as an emblem of modern dance and modern culture. Angelika Reichmann takes up the issue of the influence on John Cowper of Dostoevsky, deploying the psychoanalytic thinking of Julia Kristeva to further explore the place of the abject in Powys's novels. There is nothing repetitive or even much that's familiar in these approaches, both of which demonstrate the need to read John Cowper not only within the contexts and traditions that he elected as his own, but also beyond those, in the contexts which give significance to our own pleasures of reading. It is to be hoped that the publication of John Cowper's letters to such eminent yet divergent correspondents as Dorothy M. Richardson and Emma Goldman (also reviewed here) will extend the sense of what's relevant to the Journal's concerns, and thus bring the Powyses more visibly within the horizon of students of modern culture.

Of the contributions not on John Cowper, the most substantial in this volume is the first publication of a remarkable play by T. F. Powys, 'The Wood'. Given the nature of the dialogue in TFP's fiction, one would not expect the witty repartee or learned argument such as one finds in Wilde or Shaw. There is some attempt at rustic humour in the line of Hardy, here as in the fiction; but what is remarkable about this play is its affinity to the Symbolist drama of Maeterlinck, and to the ritualized utterances that take the place of dialogue in the plays of W. B. Yeats and J. M. Synge. While we hardly expect 'The Wood' to be produced professionally, readers will be grateful to the play's editor, Elaine Mencher, for providing the evidence of TFP's familiarity with contemporary drama. We may be encouraged to think of his novels and stories as in some respects staged: that might have been a source of Samuel Beckett's interest, and would thus support the evidence presented by James Knowlson (in *The Powys Journal* XVIII) of an allusion to *Mr. Tasker's Gods* in (of all places—or, of course?) *Krapp's Last Tape*.

Louise de Bruin has rescued from obscurity a writing woman, Vera Wainwright, hitherto barely detectable in the margins of Theodore Powys's life at Mappowder. An essay such as this, scrupulously following clues in the published material, and turning up some material that's unpublished, should lead to further discoveries, for Theodore Powys was not the only interesting figure in whose shadow Vera Wainwright seems to have chosen to live, not out of shrinking, but out of a wry and wary defiance of what was expected of her. (See photographs on pages 11 and 66.)

The good news is that 'the Cult of Powys'—as celebrated in our opening essay, a piece that has waited over sixty years to be printed and that describes a visit to Phudd Bottom eighty years ago—continues to thrive, yet becomes less and less cult-like. That openness is exemplified by the international range of our contributors; one of our contributors writing on John Cowper is an academic in France, another teaches at a Hungarian university, and a third is based in Tunisia. And this without any of our customary reliance on Scandinavia (the Contributing Editor excepted).

To Elaine Mencher we are indebted not just for the text of Theodore's play but for the thorough presentation by high-wire techno-typography of the process of its composition and revision. One can hardly resist voicing the hope that 'The Wood' might still be seen for all those fallen trees—the signs of erasure. This is not unrelated to the editorial matter indicated by our frontispiece illustration of one of the letters from John Cowper to Dorothy Richardson. How to represent manuscript in print? That is the fundamental question for all editing, and over the years the editors have enjoyed debates and disputes with our long-serving type-setter (and Publications Manager), Stephen Powys Marks. Should the printed text be true to the vagaries of script, or should it sacrifice the trees in order for the textual wood to be made clearly legible? Different purposes demand a variety of solutions. When presenting primary texts, original material hitherto unpublished, we endeavour to be maximally faithful (within the ever-expanding limits of typography) to the manuscript; when citing such material within a scholarly essay our practice is to bring manuscript into conformity with standard conventions. We owe much to Stephen Powys Marks, and also to Louise de Bruin, on whose powers of proof-reading we continue to rely, gratefully. The elegance of *The Powys Journal* is impressive: the Journal ought to attract readers on its aesthetic merits alone, and every year the editors look forward to receiving material worthy of such distinguished textual embodiment.

The editors, the Editor: Richard Maxwell has been a familiar figure at Powys conferences in Britain and North America over the past twenty-five years, and is widely known as a scholar not only of Powys but of historical fiction. A major work *The Historical Novel in Europe, 1650–1950* appeared in 2009. Those who attended the Conference last summer in Llangollen will have appreciated and enjoyed Richard's presence, his wit, enthusiasm and sharp sense of wonder. His wife and son were also of the company, enhancing and enriching our days under the craggy protection of Dinas Brân. It was a shock of particular force to learn shortly afterwards that Richard had been diagnosed with a brain tumour, and that the prognosis was not good. He at once resigned his teaching duties at Yale University, and asked the Contributing Editor to take over his editorial responsibilities on *The Powys Journal*. One would like to think that even more work than usual has gone into this volume, if only to produce one that matches the standard set by Richard over the past two years; and to produce an issue that expresses something of our affection, admiration and gratitude. Richard has continued to write in recent months, with difficulty, and it is a special honour for us to include his short essay on the motif of 'the iron bar', from Scott to Powys. To Richard, his wife Katie Trumpener and their son Alexander, the Contributing Editor offers this issue, along with the Society's dearest wishes.

CL

Vera Wainwright as a young woman.
© April Parks *(See article on page 144.)*

MELVON L. ANKENY

Evans Rodgers: The Cult of Powys

The typescript of 'The Cult of Powys' was found in the Lloyd Emerson Siberell Papers, Rare Books and Manuscripts Library, the Ohio State University Libraries. The first section was slated for publication in *The Outrider: A Journal for the Civilized Minority* (1933–34) but the journal ceased before publication. With the addition of a 'Second Movement' and presumably with the current title now added, it was to appear in Siberell's own publication, *Imprimatur*. But that publication also ceased (in 1947) prior to the article's publication.

'The Cult of Powys' was written by Evans Rodgers, a young 'disciple' of John Cowper Powys. Little is known about him aside from specific entries in JCP's diaries (*The Diary of John Cowper Powys 1931*, Kwintner, 1990; and the unpublished Diaries, courtesy of Morine Krissdóttir). Rodgers was born in 1905 in Baltimore, Maryland and the 1910 United States Federal Census gives his name as Isaac E. Rodgers, Jr. By the time he graduated from Johns Hopkins University in 1928, he was known as Evans Rodgers.

The first section of 'The Cult of Powys' details the experience of visiting JCP in upstate New York. Phyllis Playter (the T.T.) was particularly charmed by Rodgers and empathetic to one of the characters in a novel which he was writing. 'Especially because the "unhappiness" of the young man & the breaking down of his mind seems to be the same as what she herself has suffered from in times long past.' (Diary: 10 August 1931) This novel was refused by Knopf in 1932. In August of 1932, Rodgers again visited JCP (and the Fickes) with his English bride, Joan Forester. He shared the first chapters of a new novel, *A Fair Saint* which JCP noted as 'rather thin but had some merit'. He advised Rodgers to 'exploit what <u>he knew</u> by heart from experience. The clashes of a new-married man & woman trying to reach a modus Vivendi in a new ménage.' (Diary: 11 August 1932)

Rodgers again visited briefly in August 1933, but by October of that year he had reached a point of crisis in his life. 'We had a terribly sad letter from Evans Rodgers whose nerves are at the breaking-point like the luckless hero of his own book. He has a job in Washington & cannot bear it.' (Diary: 20 October 1933) Another sad letter in November from Rodgers and 'the T.T. does so understand this nervous breakdown of his for she went through it all when she was unhappy.' This precipitated an offer whereby 'Mr. Rodgers the poor neurotic lad is to stay with us for a week coming on Dec. 7th. This was solely & entirely the idea of the T.T.; for well does she know what it is to suffer this way!' (Diary: 9 & 28 November 1933) Rodgers was acknowledged to be the 'perfect guest' and left them in 'very good spirits'. For a while in 1934 his fortunes seemed to improve with a new job in Washington with the National Recovery Administration and he also conceived an enthusiastic plan of collecting JCP's letters for publication after his death, which JCP countermanded.

In 1935 JCP & Phyllis now living in Corwen, Wales, learned that Rodgers's increasing mental health problems had necessitated a stay in 'that Baltimore Mad-house or rather Home for the mentally Defective where [I] went once to see Old Arnold [Shaw?]. ... He says they say he has Manic Elation or Manic Depression or one after the other.' (Diary: 16 Sept. 1935) A later 'most Agitating Letter from Evans Rodgers now separated from Joan & not at all recovered from his Manic attack suggest[ed] that he should come & live near us here.' But this was perceived to be an untenable suggestion by Powys, who thought it 'a mistake to follow his separated wife to the British Isles'. (Diary: 19 Oct. 1935) JCP then invoked his ritualistic manner and 'Put head in the Dee and prayed for the T.T. & also (later) for Evans Rodgers who in his insane state we are too selfish to invite here to be on our hands!' (Diary: 21 Oct. 1935)

In February 1936, JCP received 'A nice long happy letter from Evans Rodgers. He is quite "Normal" again.' (Diary: 28 Feb. 1936) Sporadic correspondence from Rodgers occurred over the ensuing years including news of a position at the *New Orleans Item* in 1945. (The longer version of 'The Cult of Powys' was submitted to Siberell from New

Orleans.) In 1954 there are several JCP Diary entries noting letters from Rodgers now using his full name of 'Isaac Evans Rodgers', but after that nothing more appears.

Rodgers's former wife, Joan, maintained some contact with JCP and Phyllis in England. She went on to have an interesting career as a founding member of the Astrological Association of Great Britain in 1958 and as editor of their *Astrological Journal* for a period. In 1960 her book, *The Art of Astrology*, was published by H. Jenkins. In a letter to Phyllis, Joan Rodgers (referring to her former husband as 'Billy'!) wrote: 'It seems so strange to think that Billy was always struggling to appear in print (in my time—perhaps he has published the great American novel since?) & I who did not think of it, except in astrological journals, should have it laid at my feet. It was nice to get news of Billy. As I expect you know, we never correspond: the whole subject was too painful to me for a number of years; but now thank heaven, it has all worn off with the passage of time. Indeed, I sometimes wonder if I bear any resemblance to the young person you met so long ago in New York State!' (4 July 1961—letter courtesy of Morine Krissdóttir)

It is hoped that, wherever his life led him, Evans Rodgers (or Isaac, or Billy) would have been pleased that 'The Cult of Powys' has at last appeared in print.

From: Mr. Evans Rodgers
The New Orleans Item
New Orleans, La.

THE CULT OF POWYS

In August, 1929 a friend went into a book-store and asked the clerk if he had any new long novels. The clerk asked what sort of novel; and this friend of mine, who was buying me a present for my twenty-fourth birthday, said: "That doesn't matter. This fellow just likes long novels."

It was through this rather peculiar way of buying a book that I soon held in my hands John Cowper Powys' huge novel Wolf Solent. My copy is the first London edition, bound in green boards, and I shall never forget how fascinated I was with the gold stamping on its spine: those mysterious words, Wolf Solent, - that strange last name, Powys.

For a long time I mispronounced this name by following the spelling, a foolish thing to do with Welsh names; and it was not until two years later, when I met Mr. Powys, that I learned that he pronounced it John Cooper Poe-iss. Meanwhile, he had become; and he remains, the chief hero of my life.

For a year I went on a real Powys jag, reading with uncontrolled enthusiasm every line he had ever written; and finally I could no longer resist the urge to tell this man, whoever he might be, that every word of his works seemed written specially and directly to me. It was my first fan letter to an author; and I dropped it in the box in trembling fear that I would appear ridiculous in his eyes. How little I knew then of his character!

By return mail came these comforting, exciting words to me:

"I was simply thrilled by your noble letter . . . I fancy you too must have Welsh blood in your veins, sir, or you could hardly have got the particular line of reaction to life, which I tried to convey, so clearly - just as if you knew by instinct where this very devious stream flowed; round what rocks and under what rocks, thro' what salt marshes, and into the sea by what a channel!"

The first minor miracle had happened between Powys and me, for I was astounded to realize that his hand was quite like my own! A few months later I was startled to read in his third letter to me: "Your interest in my ideas has been an encouragement to me ever since I first saw your hand . . . the hand of someone, I would say at random, who knew Greek!"

I had had my first taste of Powys' elegant, subtle flattery, and I loved it. My knowledge of Greek stopped short at the names of college fraternities, but this I kept a dark secret from him - he himself, no doubt, was a Greek scholar; he had perhaps noticed the similarities of our hands; and had quickly made me a Greek scholar too.

Also, I enjoyed immensely his idea that Welsh blood flowed in my veins, - as erroneous, I believe, as his idea about my Greek; for only English, Scotch and Irish blood is, as far as I know, mixed in my veins. But obviously he was Welsh and it was charming flattery of him to make me Welsh too.

Meanwhile, I had dared to propose that I spend a week of my summer vacation near where he was living in Columbia County, in New York State, and had again been thrilled to have him say he was at once "making enquiries about possibilities for that week in August 24th to 31st of which you speak. Would you be prepared to pay as much as twenty dollars for board and meals included?"

Later on he gave me precise directions, in what I was to learn was the pure Powysian manner: "We are only 4-1/2 miles from Philmont (10 or 12 from Hillsdale; so that is much further away) and we are near a little hamlet called Harlemville wh. wd. be the place to make for & at the shop there they wd. tell you where I live. I am so glad you are coming, Mr. Rodgers and now I bid you so long: till we meet. . ."

There was a good deal more in this letter about how

telegrams reached him a day late; about what to do if I missed the train in New York City; and about the nearest telephone, which was in the house of one Mr. Albert Krick, who ran a "Chicken Farm" opposite the Powys establishment. But, almost needless to say, I caught the correct train, arrived at Philmont station on scheduled time, and at last beheld Mr. Powys himself, clutching a thick oak cudgel in his hand, and looking precisely like the hero of his great novel, Wolf Solent himself.

Here were eyes sunk deeper back into the skull than ever I had thought possible; here was a mass of kinky, curly graying hair; a great hook nose, a broad mouth smiling madly and Wolf's well-known weak chin. There was also a great deal of wild rubbing the hands together, of waving the huge stick through the air like the conductor of some gigantic symphony orchestra, who had lost his mind and lost his music and who at last was screaming for the musicians to forget the score and just play as loud and as hard as they could.

It was much later, several weeks after this enchanting week was over, when he was positive that my feelings would not be hurt, that he let me know of his chagrin and apprehension when he first caught sight of me. From my letters and from my hand, he said, he had expected an elderly, Greek scholar - a man of his own age, perhaps, of about 60, with whom he could converse on all the literatures of the earth. To find instead a frightened young man of 26 had been something of a shock. He did his best to put me at ease.

"Well, Mr. Rodgers! It is good to have you here at last! To hold the hand that writes so clearly! Yes! Laud we the gods, and let our crooked smokes to their blest altars rise! You'll be comfortable down the road at the Steitz farmhouse, and you'll meet my friend, my great and good friend Arthur Ficke, who only yesterday presented me with both huge red volumes of Stevenson's Home Book of Verse!"[1]

1 First published in 1912 by Henry Holt, New York.

We got into an old Ford belonging to and driven by a silent fellow of about my own age, called Carl Steitz, son of Hattie Steitz, the widowed farm-lady with whom I was to board. These three ménages - Ficke's on top of the great hill, Steitz's and Powys' in the valley below - formed a triangle of dwellings so widely different in air and atmosphere that some weeks after my visit I composed a short piece called The Manor-House, The Farm-House, and the Vicarage. But it was so intimate, so very personal, that it could be circulated only among the six or eight inhabitants of those dwellings themselves.

Soon we reached the tiny, white "toll-like" cottage where Powys lived - "lemon Verbenum, my dear Rodgers, grows in my front garden - yes, lemon Verbenum!" he was saying - "well! You come back after Mrs. Steitz gives you supper and we can talk!"

John Cowper Powys, I learned that night, is a magician, a charmer. He lives in the deepest solitude; and when he allows another human being to invade and violate that privacy so precious to him, he first charms the intruder with his conversation, weaves a circle round him thrice with the vast power of his personality; and then, with true magic, transforms him into whatever character he chooses. It happened to me, and I have eye-witnessed it happening to at least a dozen others. Apparently, he decided that since his elderly Greek scholar positively did not exist, and that with me he was dealing with a pretty literal, hard-headed factual minded fellow who could not easily be turned into any such things, - he decided, I say, that I was to be a Writer, a Novelist, a young man who promised to do what his old friend Theodore Dreiser had done, but more than that, and in finer style.

There was some slight basis of truth under what he did, for I had brought along the opening chapters of a novel I was working on. But before long he grew weary of the game with me and launched into what was nearest to his heart at the moment - the composition of his vast Glastonbury Romance.

"The title worries me, Rodgers, for when I'm in New York the subways are filled with horrible advertisements for Glastonbury underwear. Do you think that possible prospective readers will confuse my book with men's drawers?"

I said what I could to reassure him on this touchy point, but an instant later he was in dead earnest.

"My dear Rodgers, if I ever seem negligent or faulty in helping you in your gallant undertaking of writing this article about me, it is not due to lack of pride and pleasure in watching you do it, but in my entranced absorption in this enormous Glastonbury book - into which (and I give you Carte Blanche to say so) I intend to throw certain deep-sea fishings-up that I have drenched, aye! And plumbed for, in waters more remote and of wider horizons than any hitherto sailed over by me!"

Never had I heard language like this flow like a great river from the mouth of a human being; and I sat agape in that small room of his, with his mad black dog under the couch, and his white cat on his lap, and listened while his magnificent periods, like Coleridge's, I fancied, rolled on about "this duodenal ulcer that's been teasing me for years - you know I had that operation they call gasterenterostomy? - did I tell you? I expect I did; for I'm so proud of that great and grand word! Gasterenterostomy!"

Yes! This was like Samuel Taylor Coleridge. Language like this must have been the reason why Wordsworth and Charles Lamb loved Coleridge so, why even stuffy, pompous William Wordsworth put up with Coleridge's drunkenness, with his opium-eating, with all his atrocious behavior. This was why Charles Lamb died a few months after Coleridge did; simply because he could no longer breathe on an earth that could no longer hear the language of Samuel Taylor Coleridge.

But it was not until the next morning, when I joined him for his little stroll through those rolling hills of Columbia County, that I had my first real insight into this extraordinary character. He had enchanted the whole hillside.

"This old tree, Rodgers," he cried out, throwing his arms around a grey, dead trunk, "is a gossipy demon. It lives to know the news! Well! Mr. Rodgers, Mr. Evans Rodgers of Baltimore, Maryland is visiting me! That's the news!"

Then we hurried on to his Wishing Well, where he dipped his stick into the water, and waving it wildly round his head, cried, "The best of luck for Evans Rodgers!"

We went on to Merlin's Grove, a mysterious, unmarked mound of earth which was someone's grave surely; and there he chanted the prose of the Book of Common Prayer: "Man, that is born of woman, hath but a short time to live, and is full of misery. He cometh up, and is cut down, like a flower; he fleeth as it were a shadow, and never continueth in one stay. In the midst of life, we are in death …"[2]

When we got back to the cottage, I was gently told that the time had come for him to work - "WORK! My dear Rodgers, for I must earn my milk and eggs and bread with my pen! May all the gods be praised that I no longer have to lecture for my living. I was on the road, you know, lecturing for many years; and would you believe it, in one twelve-months I earned more than FIVE THOUSAND DOLLARS? But then one day a gentleman from California - who had been touched -- as you are, my friend - by my Wolf Solent - came to buy the manuscript. He sat on one side of a table and I sat on the other, opposite him. I had cut my hair close to the skull - like a convict's - so that I could feel my own skull with the inside of my own skull. And I shoved the manuscript (it was three feet high!) across the table and he had paper dollars, many green paper dollars, which he shoved my way! That's the way I like to do business. A fair trade! He wanted my sheets of paper, and I wanted his. Then I bought this place - in fee simple … lock,

2 This is given in The Bible, Job XIV, 1-2 as "Man that is born of woman is of few days, and full of trouble. He cometh forth like a flower and is cut down: he fleeth also as a shadow, and continueth not."

stock and barrel!"[3]

Drunk now, drunker than wine or whiskey would ever make me, I walked down that road, back to calm, gentle Hattie Steitz, who, in her own way, loved Mr. Powys too.

-oOo-

Second Movement

Clearly, Mr. Powys was a man with a message, a kind of reincarnation of HERMES, luck-bringing herald of the Olympian gods.

He was also, in a way, the Ancient Mariner - "till my ghastly tale is told, this heart within me burns" - and he was the Wandering Jew, tarrying till Jesus should come again. He was Ahab, chasing the white whale. He was all wanderers, all men-possessed, all men burning with the gem-like flame.

He held me, the Wedding-Guest, the listener, with his eye and skinny hand. When he first received a letter from me, he knew at once that I had heard his true voice speaking. He had written his message to me, and now, much better, he could tell me viva voce.

And what is the message from John Cowper Powys? What is his good news from the gods?

It is simple. It is simply a variation on a theme by every artist who has eaten out his heart and beat his brains against our enemies: apathy, listlessness, indifference. Gaugin [*sic*] went off to the South Seas to tell his; Beethoven signed himself BRAIN-OWNER to a Land-Owner; Richard Wagner surrounded himself with lovely, blond girls; Keats and Shelley and Byron all burned themselves up in a few thirty years; Coleridge ate opium and the reed of

3 The original 1800 page holograph manuscript of Wolf Solent was sold at this time for $1500.00 through the good offices of Arthur Davison Ficke acting as intermediary between Powys and the Pacific Coast purchaser. Later it came up for sale in a New York auction room boxed in two huge slip cases. It was sold to Lloyd Emerson Siberell, eminent Cincinnati Powys collector, and now reposes in his Powys archives at the Auburncrest Library.

William Wordsworth flattened and failed after a bright beginning.

It is hard and dangerous to try to give the message succinctly for our running readers, but the attempt must be made. Perhaps John Keats said it most clearly:

Beauty is truth, truth Beauty.

But a running-reader, the enemy, will not hear this, for it is over too quickly - only five little words!

Beauty is truth, truth Beauty.

Beethoven shrieks the message at the top of his huge voice in the opening of the Eroica; Mozart sings it with clarinets, oboes, flutes and bassoons; Vincent Van Gogh did some pretty loud yelling with his mad yellows; and gentle Jesus said it too:

Verily I say unto you, except ye become as little children, ye shall not enter the Kingdom of Heaven.

John Cowper Powys tells his with the charm of an English gentleman, the subtlety of The Renaissance Man, the cunning of a serpent .. and many hear him ..

Most of his listeners are the down-trodden, the undeserving, the misfits, the mad-men and mad-women of this Earth for whom he is the Special Champion.

His variation of the great theme has many facets, but I am inclined to believe that its heart is something like this: the only conceivable reason for life on earth is a certain kind of happiness. The Janus-headed, Good-Evil First Cause of life is utterly unconcerned with the fate and fortunes of all earthly animals; and the greatest god of all is the God of Chance. But even if you chance to be one of the ones the world considers unlucky, in that you are unsuccessful, do not despair. Happiness does not depend on success in the worldly sense at all. Indeed, success in the Powysian life is simply being happy in your own private personal way, whatever that may be.

In order to be happy, Powys suggests the unlimited development of what he calls (in his love for great and grand words) the ichthyosaurian ego.

CREDO ICHTHYOSAURIAN EGO.

The ichthyosaurus was (for the word is *obsolete*) a genus of *extinct* marine animals, combining the characters of saurian reptiles and of fishes ([ikhthuo] is Greek for fishy) with some features of whales, and having an enormous head, a tapering body, four paddles and a long tail.

How Powys resisted what must have been the great temptation to employ other ichthyo words is part of the mystery of the cult. Listen to these: *ichthyocoprolite*, the fossilized excrement of a fish... *ichthyolatry*, the worship of a fish-god, as DAGON... *ichthyomancy*, divination by means of the heads or the *entrails* of fishes...

The point of all this delightful nonsense about the ichthyosaurian ego is that Powys well knows that among his followers will be many excited, nervous, uneasy people. And he wants to persuade them to calm down, to take it easy... His trick is to suggest that deep inside all humans is a being linked and latched to some remote, *extinct* (if you please) *obsolete*, but *possible* ancestor, who lived his life lolling, dazed, half-alive, half-dead, fish-half in the deep waters and reptile-half basking in the hot sun.

And with the exertion of our own free will - his one major philosophical assumption is that we can all control our thoughts - with what he is pleased to call the ichthyosaurian *leap*, we can leave the fever and fret of everyday life, the mere drift and debris of our lives, and sink down down deep into the primordial depths of a vast peace.

We are all three beings: the sub-human, the human (all too human); and the super-human. In the dreadful middle ground of our *human* being we are competitive, aggressive, ambitious, gregarious, - qualities which tend to make us full of stress and strain, full of meanness, frustration, and unhappiness.

The great goal of happiness is to be reached only in the sub-human and the super-human egos.

A tub of hot water is a marvelous aid in finding your sub-human ichthyosaurian being. Simply shut your eyes, lie half in, half out of the water, feel the delicate differences in temperature and with a little thrust of the imagination leap back 25,000 years or so into your uralt beginnings! Now what the devil do you care whether you have money, power, or social position?

And how simple it is to slip into your super-human, your god-like being! We can all be gods at any moment we choose. Here is an easy way: help some undeserving character abundantly. Never mind about the deserving poor - leave them to the institutions of organized society, which will check up, and be sure first, and then with an eye-dropper, measure out the creature's just deserts. But you to be god-like, you remember the words of Hamlet - "use every man after his desert and who shall 'scape whipping?"

No, pick out some undeserving wretch, some drunken bum who begs you for a few pennies "for something to eat." Give him dollars for whatever he wants; and walk away with no words in exaltation! No self-respecting human being will ever do anything like this; for this is the act of a god; so you do it and be happy in your super-human ego.

You must perform these two sacred rites in the Cult of Powys - this leap into the ichthyosaurian ego, and this flight up into the super-human - with craft and cunning...in great secrecy...for if organized society finds you out, you may be locked up as a madman, and at the very least you will be marked as a queer duck, unfit for decent employment, and a person to be avoided.

But never mind about organized society! To hell with it! You must fight for your own hand, for your personal happiness, and the happiness of your loved ones.

And remember that we are all condemned to death, with but a kind of indefinite reprieve. You may die, and for all you know be gone forever, with the next breath you breathe. And you may live another day, another week, another year - we simply do not know, and we will never know, how much time is left to us. So make much of little! Take nothing for granted!

Cram pulsations into each moment as it passeth! Make a cheerful song! Be kind; be sweet; resolve to live the life of the Beautiful and the Good! If you are not in physical pain, thank all your gods that at this particular moment you are escaped from the allotment of pain for that moment which the race must somehow suffer.

Powys himself has rigorously reduced his demands and his desires so that he can live happily off the royalties which his books produce. He has a small audience, and many members of it have no money even to buy the books of their Master; and indeed, a rich, successful Powys devotee is almost a contradiction in terms.

But it doesn't matter that he is not a popular writer, with lots of money. He has maybe a hundred books, but each one is a book that he can read with joy, aloud, a hundred times.

He needs few clothes - only thick, heavy corduroy trousers, great woolen socks, big sweaters and woolen shirts to protect him against the bitter cold of winter.

His duodenal ulcer helps him in two ways: like all chronic ills, it makes him take special care of himself and thus lengthens his life; and it makes his diet so simple that its cost is nearly negligible. He lives off eggs, milk, bread, tea, honey, marmalade, and almost nothing else.

Airily, and to one who wishes to be precisely correct, maddeningly, he writes in his Autobiography - "I am so bad at dates that I forget the exact year in which I first 'set sail,' as we say, for America, but it was in the Winter - that I do know ..."

However, it must have been about 1909 when he was 37 years old; for his whole life in America took up about 25 years, and I have a letter from him dated Sept. 29th 1934 from 38 High East Street (an address he must have loved!) Dorchester, Dorset, England, written just after his return to the British Isles.

Wolf Solent was first published in 1929, so for about 20 years he was making his living at the accursed task of lecturing, the worst feature of which was the incessant traveling, specially difficult for him with his ulcer. He composed his noble "Wolf", as well as his first trial flights at the novels Wood and Stone and Ducdame on trains, in cheap rooming houses, in waiting-rooms, in restaurants, on the road. His iron determination to produce a major work in the field of the English novel - in sharp and strange contradiction to his dictum: "Cut down an ambition like the very devil," - was at last rewarded when publishers in America and England issued Wolf Solent, which I believe to be one of the six or seven finest novels in all our splendid language. And perhaps the most wonderful thing of all about this book is the mysterious gentleman from California with all his lovely green dollars who made it possible for Powys to hide away in those hills of Columbia County and fulfill his destiny to live by his pen.

The most precious book I own, of course, is my green copy of "Wolf", battered and broken, repaired and re-repaired. On the first sheet it says, in that hand that could be my own:

Few, if any, have appreciated this book more than you - but let that go! What I would like to inscribe here in indelible ink is a conjuration and incantation which will summon up out of the vasty deep powerful spirits of inspiration and continuity such as may help your Tutelary Genius as well as your Guardian Angel to steer the keel of your vessel and fill its sails as you follow your own predestined Star through the waters of your choice.

Evans Rodgers with the affte
regards & concern of his
friend
xxx John Cowper Powys

JANET FOULI

Reading Women: John Cowper Powys Dorothy M. Richardson Phyllis Playter Frances Gregg *

The books of Dorothy M. Richardson provided a focus of interest that John Cowper Powys shared with Phyllis Playter from the beginning of their companionship. His early experience of women had been various and often unhappy; raised in a Victorian vicarage, educated at public school and Cambridge, Powys was riddled with prejudices towards women. Though he was ill-prepared to understand females, there was a feminine side to his nature, recognized by Dorothy Richardson: 'Shaw claims for himself 95% femininity. If this is at all accurate, then J.C.P. and [Henry] Miller are 150% fem.: We are of course all bi-sexual, but artists of all kinds more than others.'[1] This view is corroborated by J. B. Priestley who invokes Jungian terms to assert that Powys 'was enchanted by the magic of his own unconscious. He was under the spell of one of its archetypes, the anima.'[2]

A comprehensive study of Powys's fascination with the feminine would start with his relationship towards the women in his family, and move on to his various attachments, romantic and otherwise. It would include a study of the female characters in his books. His correspondence and his diaries would have to be thoroughly scrutinized. In this essay I shall look at only a very small part of this material, focusing on John Cowper's relationship with Dorothy Richardson and her books. In doing so we will need to involve Phyllis Playter, Frances Gregg, and Richardson's husband, the artist Alan Odle.

Powys's record, as far as women are concerned, is not good. His marriage with Margaret Lyon, and eventual abandoning of her and of their son Littleton Alfred, was apparently as irresponsible as his

* *An earlier version of this paper was read at The Powys Society Conference, Llangollen, 2009.*

courtship had been. The decision to give up Frances, whom he loved, was one thing; to force her upon his friend Louis Wilkinson was something else. Such actions hardly merit the name of 'decisions': Powys appears exceptionally insensitive to the women who would have to endure the consequences of these arrangements. Linda Pashka argues 'that much of Powys's writing can be read as an attempt to display … Powys's uneasiness about, perhaps his fear of, or hatred of, women'.[3] Most of us could agree with Pashka at least over John Cowper's 'uneasiness about women'; I would suggest that his reading of Dorothy Richardson's books, in the company of Phyllis, was an attempt to come to terms with his attitude towards women and, under Phyllis's guidance, to sublimate it.[4]

Powys had been reading Dorothy Richardson for several years before the two met in the summer of 1929. In a letter to Phyllis Playter, dated 23 November 1923, Powys writes: 'I've bought Revolving Lights by Dorothy Richardson & am <u>very</u> interested in it. I will send it to you. But oh Jill it does make me long for a book by Phyllis Playter—for this excellent lady does not invent any plot—she just rambles on about anything and everything—streets and houses mostly and city trees—'.[5] In this letter Powys might have thought he was introducing Richardson's writing to Phyllis. It is however possible that Phyllis had already read some of the earlier volumes of *Pilgrimage*; in 1948 Powys told Richardson that Phyllis 'knew your books before I did!'[6] John Cowper and Phyllis may thus each have been drawn to *Pilgrimage* before they met one another. In 1920 Powys writes to Frances Gregg: 'I am reading the last volume of Dorothy Richardson's long novel which begins with Pointed Roofs. She is English, but Knopf publishes her over here. This book, "The Tunnel", in its opening chapters, follows <u>your</u> method so very closely—the same hesitant scrupulous obscurity—you must see it. Yes, I have become quiet, reserved, self-centred—a little <u>dull</u>, may-be.'[7]

In telling Frances and Phyllis about Dorothy Richardson's books, John addresses each of these women in terms of their own writing, whether actual or potential. Frances did publish some short fiction, while Phyllis had aspired to be a writer. Powys recommends *Pilgrimage* as a model for both of them. Though Frances had married Louis

Wilkinson in 1912, John Cowper remained in love with her at least until the time when he met Phyllis. Dorothy Richardson's books may have been read by Powys with both these women in mind: he had recommended her work to both women.

As early as 1907 Richardson had stated her conviction that every book can be read as 'a psychological study of the author'.[8] *Pilgrimage*, whose first volume, *Pointed Roofs*, appeared in 1915, is explicitly that, and at enormous length: a young girl leaves home and embarks on an independent forging of her own identity. In 1929, when Powys first met Richardson, she had already published nine 'chapter-volumes' of what was to become *Pilgrimage*. She would write only four more, and her progress with these is recorded in her letters to Powys. The momentum is decreasing, partly because Richardson was obliged to set her work aside in order to earn money by translating, reviewing, or editing, but there were other reasons too. In *Pilgrimage* she was making a fiction of her own life, bringing her account up to the point when she started to write about it.

Her protagonist Miriam Henderson had received, like John Cowper himself, a late-Victorian education, but had resisted attempts to make her conform to the conventional model of femininity. Born into a family of girls, she had been brought up, by her father, as the 'son' that nature had denied him, and at first she shared his contempt of women-in-general. This made her a female with some of whose views Powys could identify. *Pilgrimage* charts Miriam's slow progress towards 'fulfilment'—the last word of the final volume—and it is only when she can come to terms with herself as a woman that she can start life as a creative writer. John Cowper and Phyllis follow this progression, and if it is true that 'he reached through [Phyllis] an eventual appreciation and perception of the nature of the feminine in others—and perhaps in himself',[9] their shared and continuing reading and discussion of Richardson's books is surely a factor to be credited. Michael Ballin believes that it is through Phyllis that 'Powys acknowledges the strain of antifeminism within him'. We can only speculate on the topics of conversations between John Cowper and Phyllis; we can assume with confidence that the character and fate of Miriam Henderson would have formed some part of them.

Pilgrimage presents the experience of a woman from her own point of view: this was a revelation for Powys.[10] He recommended the different 'chapter-volumes' to his audiences as he travelled round North America lecturing on literary and cultural topics, but found that the volumes were often out of print. However, it was sometimes the case that his audiences already knew them.[11] There is no evidence that Richardson was ever the subject of a lecture,[12] but discussions after the lectures certainly included mention of her books. Powys mentions her in several of his non-fictional books written in the 1930s—notably his monograph *Dorothy M. Richardson* (1931).[13] In the *Autobiography* there is a mention of Richardson who thus represents an exception to his own rule: that the *Autobiography* was 'to be written on a very singular method. It will *contain No Women at all*—not even my Mother'.[14] However, he does mention several women, all of them at some distance from his emotional life: 'with the exception of Dorothy Richardson I feel that I owe a greater debt to Constance Garnett than to any other woman writer of our time.'[15]

Before they met, John Cowper wrote to Richardson: 'I think I may boast that I know Miss Miriam as well as I know any of the great invented characters'.[16] His recognition that Dorothy *was* Miriam must have been confirmed as soon as they met; it was obliquely admitted by Dorothy when she referred to real people by using their fictional names. For Phyllis, John wrote 'Notes at the time of first meeting—Summer '29'[17] in which Dorothy 'introduced a lovely youth of 21 as "Michael's" son—"Harriet" lives in San Antonio as Mrs Hale.' These characters have stepped out of her fiction into real life, and Powys has no difficulty in seeing Dorothy as Miriam. He may have been surprised to find that 'Miriam' was married, for one of the themes of *Pilgrimage* is Miriam's avoidance of marriage, seen as 'the sheltered life'. Miss Richardson was not only 'Miriam Henderson' but also Mrs Odle. Yet marriage to Alan Odle did not represent 'the sheltered life' for Dorothy, any more than companionship with John did for Phyllis. His remarks to Phyllis in 'Notes at the time of first meeting' serve to put Phyllis in the picture and to convey the impression of a parallel between them: 'Her room (Mr Odle's house) exactly like Patchin Place ... a dingy old house' (244) and 'I think she must be about my age'. He records Alan Odle telling him that he would have been 'dead long ago but for "Dorothy"'(243) and that Dorothy 'was very ignorant of literature before she lived with Mr. Odle' (244). Each of the Odles therefore owes something fundamental to the other. 'Mr Odle', John Cowper writes, 'was an enchanting being, fragile, delicate to the last degree—a very fine fantastic illustrator of Rabelais—and Candide—a charming wraith—hardly a human being. The story of their first meeting ... .'[18]

Marriage to Alan Odle contributed to the slowing down of Richardson's creative writing, as she had not only to cook, clean and mend for her husband whose health was fragile, but also to earn money by writing for the papers. 'The sheltered life', for her, was the conventional, socially correct life of a professional man's wife who lived in the shadow of her husband, keeping house and entertaining his friends as etiquette required. Alan did not make these demands on her, but left her free to write, as he was also free to draw. She however was the breadwinner.

Phyllis's life with John Cowper involved the abandoning of her own literary ambition, and the channelling of her creative energy into a degree of collaboration with him in the writing of his books: 'But she said at breakfast today that she got more satisfaction in her Life Illusion by helping to write Six Massive Books that we project than by "travelling about Europe".'[19] So Powys recorded in his diary. She read and discussed his books as he was writing them, often initiating revision, and Powys respected, even relied upon her advice. On Saturday 3 May 1930 we find this entry: 'I began a rather feeble essay on Dorothy Richardson. The T.T. will improve it later on.' Powys compares Phyllis with Richardson and the American Ruth Suckow (1892–1960): 'The T.T. has a critical penetration ... that is *just* as good—& *better* in many ways—than either of these mistresses of the art!' (Diary, Monday 25 January 1932).[20] To Richardson he wrote 'I can't *tell* you what a help Phyllis is to me in my writings. She *won't* let things pass; that are carelessly written from the top of my brain ... .'[21] Throughout his diary he records Phyllis's constant collaboration, and their close discussion of his fiction.

It took Richardson four years to complete her tenth volume, *Dawn's*

Left Hand (1931), and part of her slowing-down is due to her feelings about the events there recorded: in particular, she relates Miriam's meeting with Amabel and the development of a very close friendship—the first and only really close friendship she would have with another woman. This volume is crucial to *Pilgrimage* because it shows Miriam coming to terms with her femininity after having always been treated as her family's 'longed-for son' (*Revolving Lights*, 250), and thus assuming her father's contempt of women. Amabel educates her and gives her insights into feminine nature. The following volume, *Clear Horizon*, which took a further four years to write, relates the way in which Miriam avoids both marriage and an importunate friendship: her friend Michael Shatov had proposed to her, and Amabel was becoming jealous of her independence. Miriam suggested that they marry each other. United in their love for her, and trusting her implicitly, they do so. Miriam had realized that marriage with Michael would be a disaster and, moreover, that if she married, she would forfeit her freedom to become a writer.

The fiction is a re-working of fact. In 1906, Dorothy Richardson had met Veronica Leslie-Jones, and a year later, Veronica had married Dorothy's friend Benjamin Grad, in circumstances very similar to those of Amabel and Michael. They remained friends with Richardson, and indeed bought Dorothy's wedding ring in 1917 when she married Alan Odle. But they had been unhappy and had separated in 1927, at the time when Richardson was starting to write *Dawn's Left Hand*.

In *Pilgrimage* Richardson expressed her debt to Veronica. Her fictional representation, Amabel, is a catalyst, working to complete the action of Miriam's other friends, those who in some way contributed to her development as a writer. It is with Amabel that Miriam reaches full acceptance of her femininity, a condition that was necessary before she could achieve complete independence. After meeting Amabel, Miriam can say: 'The desire to commit oneself came from the sense of having, at last, an available identity.' This is to be found in *Dimple Hill*,[22] the volume of *Pilgrimage* dedicated to John Cowper Powys, who had himself written in the *Autobiography* (1934): 'Yes, I certainly have realized my identity in these New York hills'.[23] It was there that he first lived with Phyllis Playter, and he may indirectly be attributing his self-awareness to her; is Miriam's realization of 'an available identity' through Amabel in some respects to be seen as patterned on John and Phyllis? The wedding of Amabel and Michael is evoked in one of the last chapters of this volume dedicated to John Cowper Powys. The final chapter-volume of Pilgrimage is *March Moonlight*, of which parts were published serially in *Life and Letters* through 1946, though it did not appear as a volume until 1967. Its last chapter, with which the entire *Pilgrimage* is concluded, presents Miriam holding Amabel and Michael's baby. Miriam is now starting to write; the leitmotif of the Madonna and the title of *Pilgrimage*, which gives form and direction to Miriam's life and evokes her quest for a vocation, may suggest that the baby is a symbol of the book itself: the baby is both biological, the child of the Shatovs, and, figuratively, a sacred symbol, the child of the Madonna.

Powys had extricated himself from a marriage that confined him. He had left his wife Margaret and their son Littleton Alfred, when he went to lecture in North America. He justifies himself in his *Autobiography*:

> In the first place it would not have been possible 'to keep Burpham going,' and to give my son the education, at Sherborne and Corpus, that my great-grandfather had given my grandfather … had I confined my services to the Extension work at home. In the second place my life in trains and hotels … was a grand escape from all those worries in English social life to which … I was peculiarly alive.[24]

In the United States in 1912 Powys met and fell deeply in love with Frances Gregg, but as he was already married and his wife would not divorce him, there could be no question of marriage.[25] However, he thought he had found a solution, in the words of the child born to Wilkinson and Frances Gregg: 'It was because Jack could not marry Frances that he thought it an excellent idea to marry her to his great friend and fellow-lecturer, Louis Wilkinson. It was also a way by which he could keep Frances near him.'[26]

This marriage caused great unhappiness and ended in disaster. Frances and Louis went to England and eventually divorced, in

1922. Announcing the divorce, Frances wrote to Jack: 'You are not responsible for us, my dear'.[27] A year later, Powys met Phyllis Playter, and they soon began to live together in New York; but he continued to write to Frances and to send her occasional sums of money. Frances's son Oliver was his godson, and John Cowper always took a very close interest in him, just as Richardson did in David Grad. The son of Veronica and Benjamin Grad, David (born 1909) was present in June 1929 when Powys first called on Richardson.[28]

The separation of Veronica and Benjamin Grad was a major factor in the breakdown that Richardson suffered in 1934, while writing *Clear Horizon* (1935). It was in *Clear Horizon* that Miriam suggests to Amabel that she should marry Michael, even though Miriam realizes the absurdity of this union: 'Not merely difficult and sacrificial and yet possible. Simply impossible. With her unlocated, half-foreign being, Amabel could see nothing of the impossibility of spending one's life in Jewry' (*Clear Horizon*, 292). Powys had guessed something was wrong two or three years beforehand, while the breakdown was 'incubating': 'I do hope & pray that you & Mr Alan are all right. I get anxious about you sometimes. I showed your handwriting to an Expert Graphologist (if that's the word for it) & he said "this person is living at a terrific tension & strain of nerves".'[29]

Richardson's involvement with Benjamin and Veronica Grad was awkwardly deepened by their fictional representation in *Pilgrimage*; her friendship with each of them survived their own marital difficulties and separation. Richardson salves her conscience by not only recording events but by giving us (as if herself confessing) the intimate thoughts of Miriam; through Miriam we can sense Dorothy's awareness of the unhappiness she had caused, along with the need to preserve her own independence. Miriam is mean, disloyal and selfish; the reader of *Pilgrimage* is divided between several parameters of judgement. The moral code would condemn Miriam; but this condemnation should be deferred, since Miriam is continuing to develop and the narrative is incomplete. In this fiction, the telling of the act is like a confession, and according to Freud and others, any confession invites the complicity of the person who hears or reads it. Guilt tends therefore to be shared, and the reader's faculty of judgement is correspondingly weakened. When the guilty person becomes the author of a fictional rendering of the guilty act, this act is held at a distance, and its author achieves some degree of immunity. The distinction between author and actor is protective: Powys's *Autobiography* gives to the portrayal of its protagonist a fictional quality that protects its author. In 1948 Gaston Bachelard wrote: 'Ecrire, c'est se cacher',[30] and Foucault expressed the same idea in 1969: 'I am no doubt not the only one who writes in order to have no face.'[31]

When Powys began to read the chapter-volumes of *Pilgrimage* he could not know how they would develop. His own nearest attempt at autobiographical fiction, *After My Fashion*, was written in 1919–20 but was published only posthumously, in 1980.[32] Powys mentions its writing in a letter to Frances Gregg of October 1920; in August 1921 he tells Frances that 'last summer's rotten novel of mine cannot find a publisher',[33] and that Llewelyn 'condemned it even worse than you'.[34] This is evidence that Frances had read and criticized *After My Fashion*. Powys made no further attempts to find a publisher for it.

Frances's comments on Powys's books were sharply critical: from the start of his career as a novelist she and Louis disliked and mocked John Cowper's books. Louis's *Blasphemy and Religion* (1916) compared *Wood and Stone* unfavourably with Theodore Powys's *Soliloquy of a Hermit*; this brief pastiche was accompanied in 1916 by *The Buffoon*, a long *roman à clé* in which John Cowper is ridiculed as 'Jack Welsh'. Frances's criticism of the early novels has not survived, but Powys's letters to her sometimes refer to it:

> As to your stricture upon Rodmoor, my brain isn't capable at this moment of any defence—though I feel obscurely that such a defence may be set up. But I never was able to deal with your fierce attacks. They always leave me—hit—puzzled—bewildered—and with a sort of hopeless wish that there were such a thing as the Judgement Day.[35]

Twenty years later, Frances was charmed by the title of *Maiden Castle* when she received an advance copy as a Christmas present in 1936, but when she read it, she wrote another 'fierce attack', at great length, accusing the author of childishness and an abysmal lack of imagination.[36] Later still, on receiving *Morwyn*, Frances wrote: 'I am not your audience, most plausible Lucifer', though by way of concession she added: 'You are a great artist.'[37] The complexity of her response is indicated in another letter: 'It is a strange thing that no matter how grieved and alienated I may, myself be, by your writings, I am, as well, like any tender mother, so pleased and thrilled when I hear you praised.'[38] Frances is however unambivalently delighted by *The Pleasures of Literature* (1938) which prompts her to declare that *Visions and Revisions* (1915) and *Suspended Judgments* (1915) had been 'my favourites of all your books'.[39]

Frances's main objection concerns John Cowper's understanding of women. In *The Art of Happiness* (1935), two chapters—nearly one-third of the book—are devoted to the relationship between men and women. Frances berates him severely for his ignorance of women:

> I wish that you would speak more guardedly of women. You know that I do not like them really, so that I am no sentimentalist pleading for the frail. I only say that you know nothing about them, and for your own dignity's sake should use a shade more discretion in writing of them. What, actually, when it comes to it, do you know of women, except of such strange harlots as we who have come your way.[40]

In the same letter she writes: 'You will think that this is a poor return for your gentleness in sending me the book . . . . Yet it is my love. I will never speak to you except truly.'

John Cowper read *The Art of Happiness* to Phyllis as he was writing it, and he records her reaction to the concluding chapter in his diary: '. . . she suddenly began to cry & then became very heart-broken & said that my cherished Philosophy was a Reaction . . . from living with her & against her ideas & ways of feeling as—she said—happened with all men and women. I denied this & explained the deep truth that it was my Protection against Reality & Responsibility.'[41] At that time, Phyllis was still adjusting to life in England, and was often very unhappy. But the emotional nature of this outburst was exceptional; for once she neither agreed with, nor approved, what he had written. There is no reference to *The Art of Happiness* in the correspondence with Dorothy Richardson, who presumably did not read it and did not enter into the debate that arose from it. Frances and Phyllis had both, at different times, been intimate with John Cowper, so they had good reason to be upset that his relationship with them had still left him with ideas that they found alien.

John Cowper was puzzled by their reactions. Frances tried hard to help him to understand, sending him a book cover that she had embroidered:

> I was using it to try to get hold of something that gave meaning to the word love. You said that no one had ever answered you as to what it meant. I don't wonder. It is the whole crux of the mystery. But something of mine [i.e. the embroidery] might strike fire in your brain so that you found out the mystery for yourself.[42]

Her last extant letter to John Cowper fittingly puts love (and their love) in perspective, and in a narrative that would be closed by Frances's death in the bombardment of Plymouth in the autumn of 1941:

> I was not angry with you, but your letter reminded me of the old sad years when I was, I suppose, loved, but when I wanted to think, and to be understood. Being loved was only the second best. I used to take it in a fury of trying to forget the things that were really at my heart. There have to be lovers, but it is dangerous not to understand a woman and not to know her as she really is.[43]

* * * *

The complaint of both Frances and Phyllis, directed against John Cowper, was yet extended to allow that men in general fail to understand women. This would have struck a chord with Dorothy Richardson. Indeed, it is a theme that runs through *Pilgrimage*: Miriam is misunderstood. From the start, men assume that a single woman must be in need of a husband, and Miriam has to extricate herself from a number of near-engagements. She is told by one of her suitors: 'You misrepresent yourself most tremendously.'[44] The suitor who tells her this encourages her to write, but adds: 'Perhaps the novel's not your form. Women ought to be good novelists. But they write best about their own experiences. Love-affairs and so forth. They lack creative imagination.'[45] With this sweeping statement, Miriam is humiliated, and the resemblance between Miriam and her author is at once implied and mocked. Miriam keeps to herself this thought: 'a lifetime might well be spent in annotating the male novelists, filling out the vast oblivions in them'. And Frances might have concurred: for whose oblivions are vaster than John Cowper's?

Richardson did of course write about her own experiences, not through any limitation but with the purpose of correcting an imbalance. She was 'attempting to produce a feminine equivalent of the current masculine realism'.[46] The critical history of *Pilgrimage* is as much a saga of misunderstanding as is the life of its protagonist. Powys tried to correct that in his *Dorothy M. Richardson* in 1931. Yet just a year after this came out, Richardson would be criticizing his own understanding of women. That letter is missing, but Powys records it in his diary: 'A letter about my book [*A Glastonbury Romance*] from Dorothy Richardson. She liked it! But quarrels over my description of what women's feelings are in love. ...'[47]

Having already invited Richardson to criticize *Wolf Solent* (which she did at length, and favourably),[48] he is puzzled by her comments on *A Glastonbury Romance*, and his reaction is a confusing tissue of metaphor and classical allusion that entirely evades the issue.[49] Criticism of one's books is a sensitive matter to any writer, for as Richardson often says, in her own voice and in that of Miriam: 'In a book the author was there in every word.'[50] Alan Odle uses a pictorial metaphor to express his praise of Powys's *Autobiography*:

> Alan has read the whole of your book with the engrossed delight he gives to so very little modern work, & has, as usual when reading you, bombarded me with fragments. Using his own dialect, he declares that the way you have chosen is the right way to do a 'full-length'.[51]

Alan was in fact the ideal reader, 'the very kindest & most horoscopically akin reader of all I can catch the sleeves of'.[52] His praise was usually expressed in Dorothy's letters, to strategic purpose: 'Alan loved his work and behind him, eagerly reading, I used to hide by quoting A., my own difficulty in getting through anything beyond "Wolf Solent", bits of "Glastonbury" and "The Pleasures of Literature", embodying his life-work as lecturer and, for me, his one solid contribution.'[53] Dorothy Richardson thus shares with Frances Gregg a marked preference for John Cowper's literary essays over his novels. Powys revelled in Odle's praise, as reported by his wife, in this case of *A Glastonbury Romance:*

> What a thing it is for me to have a reader like he is! I knew he'd like it! I knew it wd hit his peculiar humour & imagination; for I know his twist of mind a bit, really, by seeing him that time, by what you have said, & by his surprising drawings. Its wonderful to me to have safe & sound a kind spirit like he is to depend on for general effects & not be bothered by casual slips, 'bricks' dropt, & other shortcomings but just enjoying what suits his mood in unqualified freedom from what frets or jars or so easily might if he read captiously or maliciously and not only to have such an one but have him so securely lodged at the side of my own favourite modern writer! What a piece of luck.[54]

Alan himself wrote only two letters to Powys, expressing his enjoyment of *Maiden Castle* and *Owen Glendower*. It required strong feelings for him to put pen to paper, and even these two were enclosed with letters from his wife.[55] He offered to contribute illustrations to two of Powys's books, *Morwyn* and *Rabelais*, though the publishers chose not to use them. To that end, an advance copy of *Morwyn* had been sent to Odle, and it was read with care by Dorothy, as she told John Cowper: 'Meanwhile wishing, yearning to contribute what I can to your blessed book, I've read it with the wily eye of the proof-reader.'[56] She had praised the book 'off her own bat', and spent time reading it carefully and thoroughly, and suggesting corrections. These he acknowledges, though he then prevaricates and is reluctant to use them. It was, he wrote in his diary, 'like Charlotte Bronte correcting the works of Mr Peacock or of Harrison Ainsworth!' and in the end he incorporated none of Dorothy's suggestions, 'for I like my *slip-shod* style. I *deliberately* use it!'[57]

Frances's reaction to *Morwyn* was, as we have seen, unfavourable: 'I am not your audience, most plausible Lucifer, and even my ideals of moral courage do not demand such witless heroism as reading a book like this.'[58] Yet she may have contributed to Powys's idea for the book when, in December 1936, she told him of a story she had written 'all about a little Welsh girl and her dog'.[59]

Phyllis is present in *Morwyn* as 'the little Welsh girl' with her dog. There is no record in John Cowper's diaries that Phyllis read the manuscript while he was writing the story, though she did this with his other fiction, making suggestions that he took into account, often rewriting passages and even chapters. There is little reason to suppose that Phyllis was not as closely involved in the composition of *Morwyn*. Among all John Cowper's books *Morwyn* is singular, for it is a book in whose theme and composition we can trace the involvement of John Cowper Powys and Phyllis Playter, and of Alan Odle and Dorothy Richardson.

Collaboration in art is the exception rather than the rule. Phyllis was in a privileged position because she had John Cowper's entire confidence. Under her influence he would make structural changes to *A Glastonbury Romance*, *Weymouth Sands* and *Maiden Castle*, and one wonders if she also improved the sort of writing that Richardson wanted to correct in *Morwyn*. John Cowper does not allow Richardson such direct and intimate ingress into his work-in-progress, but he does repeatedly claim that she influenced his work in a less direct manner. In writing his *Autobiography*, he tells Richardson that 'I am copying *you*—in the sense of trying to give not quite "imperfectly realized" *surroundings*!'[60] Her influence does not stop at the fictional rendering of autobiography: the same phrase occurs in his diary two years later: '*Worked hard* at Chapter VIII [of *Maiden Castle*] wh is a very important chapter from my own private point of view—& lets trust that the reading of our friend Dorothy Richardson's Clear Horizon has given me a greater scrupulously serious attempt to avoid *Imperfect Realization*!'[61] John Cowper was aware of how Dorothy Richardson would write 'I. R.' (for 'Imperfect Realization') in the margins of her manuscripts when she was dissatisfied with what she had written; when the writing of one of his books coincided with his reading of one of hers, Powys would try to match her quality of writing and intensity of purpose, as the Diaries attest.

What is the connection between the long penultimate chapter of *Maiden Castle* and *Clear Horizon*? 'Midsummer's Eve' is packed with action that involves most of the characters in *Maiden Castle* before the concluding chapter brings them 'full circle'. Richardson's books are written in a quite different mode. Yet *Clear Horizon* has some affinity with this dramatic chapter of *Maiden Castle*, for in it she brings together the major influences of Miriam's London years and 'clears the horizon' for Miriam to leave London and move towards her goal. Chapter 3 of *Dimple Hill* (dedicated to Powys) opens with Miriam reflecting: 'The worlds from which one after another she had retreated, gathered round her redeemed from bondage to time and place, each, now, offering a brimming cup her unsteady hands had been unable to hold, each showing as a most desirable dwelling-place.'[62]

What John Cowper gleans from Richardson's books—formally, aesthetically at the antipodes of his own—is insight into feminine nature; in this he further gains enormously by reading and discussing the books of *Pilgrimage* with Phyllis. Influence can also be seen in the matter of style. In aspiring to learn from Richardson's, John Cowper could also be critical:

> Coming to my own discursive & fantastic Dorchester Romance after reading [*Clear Horizon*] I find I can't help trying—of course in vain! to get *something* of its quality—of things *not* 'imperfectly realized' as they pass.... [Comparing *Clear Horizon* with the two preceding volumes of *Pilgrimage*] one thing I must rush to say & that is that the style seems so much more firm subtle and winnowed ....[63]

Richardson never read the diary entry in which we see the impact her book made on John and Phyllis:

> After tea the T.T. read to me the *End of Dorothy Richardson's Book*.... Then I asked her to read aloud to me a page or two of *Dorothy Richardson's Clear Horizon* wh she did & we talked happily of the

> difference in Miriam from her early prudish old-maidish state to now—going to have a child in regular Greenwich Village style—& all her lovers 'Hypo', 'Michael', Densley the Doctor—all put aside for the secret of her individualistic *Sacred Profanity*— [64]

Here Powys anticipates the direction *Pilgrimage* is taking. Any pilgrimage is a journey to a shrine, though the precise nature of this one will not be revealed until the posthumous publication of the thirteenth 'chapter', *March Moonlight*, in 1967. John Cowper and Phyllis were receptive readers, helped perhaps by their habit of reading her books to each other: 'Dorothy, I've just finished reading aloud Dawn's Left Hand. … We finished it in about four nights, *going slow* as should ever be with your works … .'[65] He continues:

> I seem to see a thrilling book of short critical essays by D.M.R. on the theme, 'what the great Novelists *leave out*'.
>
> It would never do I guess to spare the time from the *next* chapter—but I can't help being so sure that a book of critical essays (writ in a style that was a compromise between your academic 'pot-boiling' manner & your immortal manner) would not only be caviare, something very special in virtuosity, to the 'elect', but also sell well & *make money* with the Generality![66]

She never did write such a book. It was John Cowper who did, in 1938, with *The Pleasures of Literature*, the book that enjoyed the admiration of both Dorothy Richardson and Frances Gregg.

Writing requires solitude, and this might seem difficult to achieve when the writer is married. Yet both the Odles and John Cowper and Phyllis enjoyed secure relationships that nevertheless gave them the freedom and solitude they needed. The lives of both couples followed a strict routine in which the needs of each one were respected. Writing just after the death of Alan, Dorothy defined their relationship as a '*solitude à deux*' even '*égoisme à deux*'.[67] In November 1946 she had published in *Life and Letters* 51 a chapter of what was to become *March Moonlight*. Powys comments on what she writes there about marriage:

> And oh Miriam Miriam!—what a tragic sentence is this?
> '*the loss of unthreatened solitude*' God! you do understand things!

> Phyllis has taught me & I have repeated it like a Monk telling Beads that *to keep Solitude at the bottom of Pandora's Box* is the secret of that Platonic Symposiacal Man- & Woman *symbolic* Figure—cut in gold—& worn in Gargantua's Cap! for each as it thinks of the other (seeking its own most cunningly by seeking not its own) lets its thoughts go clear thro' the other into lovely elemental dark *empty* lonely *'unthreatened solitude'* yes yes unthreaten*able* solitude now that the secret of life à deux is caught on the wing & *let go again* so that *both* can always *go away.*[68]

Marriage and solitude are seen here as compatible: the *solitude à deux* that is the experience both of the Odles and John and Phyllis is the ideal situation for all of them. Each of them respected the 'life-illusion' of the companion, in spite of apparent incompatibilities. Powys, coming to meet Richardson in 1929, was astonished by Alan's drawings, so utterly different from his wife's fiction. So it is by dissonance or lack of sharing that the 'life-illusion' is identified as the sacred self that must be preserved, and that must be protected from others, even from the loving Other. Discussing Frances with Phyllis, Powys concluded that it was her violation of the 'life-illusion' of others that had led to her isolation:

> At breakfast the T. T. asked me why it was that after Louis, Lulu & myself had been so stirred and rattled by Frances, that we could go on & relegate her so coolly to a place on the remote horizon. I said it was because the deepest instinct in all men is their secret Life Illusion of Themselves .... Frances attacked this inner self this deep inner self or life-illusion habitually; & thus all three of us have had to grow a sort of protective fibre round the wound she made. The strange thing is that while we have all changed, Frances has remained the same.[69]

John Cowper had written to Frances in 1921: 'You know I sometimes think that lots of our queer rages against each other come from our being most damnably and unluckily *alike* . . . .'[70] Both then and later Frances could not help expressing criticisms that John Cowper found negative and alienating.

Phyllis was able to identify the change in John Cowper since the days of his love for Frances, as recorded in his Diary for 12 March 1932:

> At Breakfast she spoke most eloquently on the subject of *Frances* and her idea is that F. has remained at the Pre-Raphaelite Epoch & has not let herself grow with the times. She said that I too had something of the Maurice Browne Epoch in my nature, but had deliberately changed my nature .... Yes, it is true. ... Thus I have, with growth of a more refined taste, & also – above *all* be it noted – having found my Little Ballad Girl ... completely re-created myself & by degrees, in my worship of the Chthonian Demeter of the British Museum & my life with the T.T., I am changing my Life-Illusion into something quieter, more earthy, more patient, more primeval, more simple.[71]

Phyllis did not criticize Powys or his books in the abrasive and negative way that, for Frances, was a mark of honesty and, we may suppose, a necessity of her own 'life-illusion'. In following Powys, first to the rural hills of New York State, then to North Wales, Phyllis showed an exceptional degree of adaptability. Did she like his calling her 'my Little Ballad Girl'? What did she really think about Powys's portrayal of women in his books? How easy was it for her to give up her own ambition to write? We do not know. Phyllis's discussions and criticisms of his books were constructive and tactful, and he set great store by her judgement, giving her his entire confidence. Their reading of Dorothy Richardson's *Pilgrimage* further strengthened the bond between them, enabling Powys to reach a greater understanding of Phyllis, and through her of the feminine.

'The eternal feminine leads us on': Goethe's Faust sold his soul to the devil for the sake of a woman. Powys found *his* woman in Phyllis. Where does the quest for the feminine lead, in terms of fictional portraits of women, and of relationships? When Frances Gregg criticized *Wolf Solent*, John Cowper recorded his reply: 'Wrote to Frances telling her that out of all of her attack on my book I would promise to remember to try & make ordinary people exciting and not pile up too many exciting people—this *was* the best of her onslaughts and it tallies with many words of the T.T.'[72] Three weeks later, writing to Dorothy Richardson, he surely anticipates, and therefore neutralizes, any similar criticism that she might make, by telling her that he could not resist the temptation 'to let myself go *to the limit* in my love of weird abnormal characters and in romantic sensuality'.[73] Yet in writing his next book, he seems to have forgotten those criticisms, or that he had promised to heed advice: 'I am writing this Glastonbury Book with extraordinary delight. Its just as if I were telling myself an exciting story of the sort I like best … .'[74]

Powys did not take the sort of advice that might have made his books palatable to Frances Gregg or to Dorothy Richardson. Alan, however, loved his novels; and Alan shared with John Cowper both shyness and a distrust of women. Richardson, brought up to share some of her father's attitudes, had once been opposed to feminism.[75] In Phyllis John Cowper had met his ideal woman, one who was 'more feminine than feminines are'; yet this is importantly qualified: '—but it was her intelligence that led her into that particular rôle'.[76] Hence the apparent contradictions in John Cowper's appreciation of Phyllis: she can be to him both a 'Little Ballad Girl' and the reader for whose critical judgement he had unbounded respect.

Dorothy Richardson was appreciated by Powys in very different terms: '… you, my friend, are like a priestess—the priestess of I-know-not-what ancient mystery—& to priestesses (as well as to priests) one instinctively, & without knowing why, finds oneself confessing.'[77] Many of his letters have a confessional character as he tells her about his 'work in progress' and asks questions about feminine attitudes; of all his correspondents, Dorothy Richardson drew from Powys a special level of respect and attentiveness. And very seldom did she answer any of his queries, as he seems to have realized; after a long sequence of questions Powys adds: 'So don't 'ee reply to this Billet Doux of Momus to the Sphinx'.[78] Like a sphinx, she keeps silence, leaving him to ponder on the testimony of Miriam, the admonitions of Frances, and the ministrations of Phyllis.

NOTES

[1] Letter of Good Friday (no year) to Henry Savage in *Powys and Dorothy Richardson: The Letters of John Cowper Powys and Dorothy Richardson*, ed. Janet Fouli (London: Cecil Woolf, 2008), 247 (Appendix 2). This volume is hereafter cited as *JCP/DMR*; the letters are identified by the numbers assigned therein, with a separate series for each of the correspondents.

[2] Introduction to John Cowper Powys, *Autobiography* (1934), (London: Macdonald, 1967) xiii.

[3] Linda Pashka, 'Powys's Punch and Judy Shows : *Weymouth Sands* and Misogyny' (*Powys Notes*, Spring 1990; reprinted in *la lettre powysienne* 12, automne 2006,) 36.

[4] JCP wrote to DMR: 'Our impatience is great to see [*Clear Horizon*] and to read it together as we have done all your "chapters" word by word with drawn-out ponderings.' *JCP/DMR*, 97 (JCP 36, 28 May 1935).

[5] Unpublished letter held in the John Cowper Powys collection, National Library of Wales, Aberystwyth.

[6] *JCP/DMR*, 232 (JCP 72, 23 December 1948).

[7] *Jack and Frances: The Love Letters of John Cowper Powys and Frances Gregg*, vol. I. Edited by Oliver Wilkinson assisted by Christopher Wilkinson (London: Cecil Woolf, 1994), 107 (Letter 94, 13 January 1920).

[8] Cited in Gloria G. Fromm, *Dorothy Richardson: A Biography* (Urbana: University of Illinois Press, 1977), 53.

[9] Michael Ballin, review of Morine Krissdóttir, *Descents of Memory: The Biography of John Cowper Powys* (New York, Woodstock; London: Overlook Duckworth, 2007), *The Powys Journal* XVIII (2008), 139.

[10] JCP often wrote to Richardson about her books: 'all my clumsy blunderings in your books have to do with—& naturally I suppose—Miriam's relations with men. Over her relations with women I hover like a sympathetic Hawk, missing very little—at least so I *think*!' *JCP/DMR*, 146 (JCP 53, 27 October 1938).

[11] As the correspondence shows, in the early 1930s JCP and Phyllis tried to find Richardson a new US publisher.

[12] He did so in a farewell lecture at the Labor Temple in New York: 'I made so much of Dorothy Richardson that Mr Simon & Schuster looked at each other and said "We must have a Conference of the Sanctum about this"—If it *does* result in their publishing *Pilgrimage* it will have made my Lectures of this crowded week *well* worth all O I pray they do.' Cited in *JCP/DMR*, 61 (Diary, 8 April 1932).

[13] London: Joiner & Steele, 1931; reprinted by the Village Press, 1974.

[14] Letter to Marian Powys Grey, 14 August 1935, quoted in *Autobiography*, xix. JCP does make passing reference to a number of women in the *Autobiography*, most of them writers.

[15] *Autobiography*, 524.

[16] *JCP/DMR*, 16 (JCP 1, 5 August 1929).

[17] *JCP/DMR*, 243-45 (Appendix).

[18] This would eventually be transcribed as Miriam's meeting with 'Mr Noble' in *March Moonlight*, though it was not published until the complete edition of *Pilgrimage* of 1967 (London: Dent; New York: Knopf); DMR had died in 1957, JCP in 1963.

[19] Friday 5 September 1930, in *Petrushka and the Dancer: The Diaries of John Cowper*

Powys 1929–1939, selected and edited by Morine Krissdóttir (Manchester: Carcanet Press 1995), 53.

20 Richardson admired Suckow; in 1939 she would be introduced to her by Powys; see Fromm, 423.

21 *JCP/DMR*, 73 (JCP 25, 31 December 1932).

22 *Dimple Hill* (1938), 424. Conveniently, all of the four-volume editions of *Pilgrimage* (Dent, Knopf, Popular Library, Virago) have the same pagination.

23 *Autobiography*, 629.

24 *Autobiography*, 506–07.

25 JCP was attracted to people with a physiognomy that he described as 'elfin-eldritch'; he used that phrase in writing to Richardson about both Phyllis (*JCP/DMR*, 56, JCP 19), and Alan Odle (*JCP/DMR*, 75, JCP 26).

26 Introduction, *Jack and Frances: the Love Letters of John Cowper Powys to Frances Gregg* vol. 1, ed. Oliver Wilkinson, assisted by Christopher Wilkinson (London: Cecil Woolf, 1994), xxvi.

27 *Jack and Frances 1*, 138 (Letter 126, May 1922).

28 See Fromm, 230.

29 *JCP/DMR*, 48 (JCP 15, 14 October 1931). DMR's nervous strain at this time was also partly due to her 'four years hard': 'the five, men's, books translated, & short stories translated & masculine continental luminaries' books commented on, have left me so rigidly set within the "rational" approach to reality that it takes more than just time to get back' *JCP/DMR*, 90 (DMR 13, 13 November 1934).

30 Gaston Bachelard, *La Terre et les Rêveries du Repos* (Paris: Conti, 1948), 320.

31 Michel Foucault, *The Archaeology of Knowledge* (London: Routledge, 1972), 177.

32 John Cowper Powys, *After My Fashion*, with a Foreword by Francis Powys (London: Pan-Picador, 1980).

33 *Jack and Frances 1*, 125 (Letter 116, 3 August 1921).

34 *Jack and Frances 1*, 144 (Letter 130, 1923).

35 *Jack and Frances 1*, 86 (Letter 71, November 1916).

36 *Jack and Frances II*, 57–58 (Letter 216, 6 December 1936).

37 *Jack and Frances II*, 95 (Letter 242, 7 October 1937).

38 *Jack and Frances II*, 97 (Letter 244, 3 November 1937).

39 *Jack and Frances II*, 140 (Letter 275, 12 November 1938).

40 *Jack and Frances II*, 26 (Letter 195, April 1935).

41 *Petrushka and the Dancer*, 176 (Friday 4 January 1935).

42 *Jack and Frances II*, 71–72 (Letter 223, 27 April 1937).

43 *Jack and Frances II*, 189 (Letter 321, 20 February 1941).

44 *Revolving Lights*, 375.

45 *Dawn's Left Hand*, 239–40.

46 Foreword to the first Dent edition of *Pilgrimage*, 1938, 9.

47 Cited in *JCP/DMR*, 64 (Diary 9 June 1932).

48 See *JCP/DMR*, 22–24 (DMR 5, 15 December 1929).

49 See *JCP/DMR*, 64–65 (JCP 22, 15 June 1932).

50 *Honeycomb*, 384. DMR identifies JCP with one of his own fictional heroes: 'You are well-pleased to become Owen Glendower. ...' *JCP/DMR*, 98 (DMR 20, 23 June 1935).

51 *JCP/DMR*, 90 (DMR 13, 13 November 1934).

52 *JCP/DMR*, 69 (JCP 23, 6 September 1932).
53 *JCP/DMR*, 247 (DMR to Henry Savage, 6 May 1951).
54 *JCP/DMR*, 62 (JCP 21, 16 May 1932).
55 Both are printed in *JCP/DMR*, p. 116 (on *Maiden Castle*. with DMR 29, 15 January 1937) and p. 193 (on *Owen Glendower*, with DMR 64, 29 October 1941). Again we see DMR using her husband's praise of JCP as a cover for her own indifference; for her view of *Owen* see her letter (12 March 1943) to Bernice Elliott: 'Did you manage to get through *Owen Glendower*? Dear John Cowper ... turns out pot-boilers with amazing rapidity.' Cited in *JCP/DMR*, 246.
56 *JCP/DMR*, 130 (DMR 36, May 1937).
57 *Petrushka and the Dancer*, 247 (23 June 1937).
58 *Jack and Frances II*, 95 (Letter 242, 7 October 1937).
59 *Jack and Frances II*, 55 (Letter 214, 3 December 1936).
60 *JCP/DMR*, 79 (JCP 27, 1 December 1933).
61 Cited in *JCP/DMR*, 101 (Diary 11 November 1935).
62 *Dimple Hill*, 424.
63 *JCP/DMR*, 102 (JCP 38, 12 November 1935).
64 Cited in *JCP/DMR*, 101 (Diary 10 November 1935).
65 *JCP/DMR*, 52 (JCP 17, 1 December 1931).
66 *JCP/DMR*, 52–53.
67 *JCP/DMR*, 227 (DMR 90, 15 March 1948).
68 *JCP/DMR*, 220 (JCP 69, 8 December 1946).
69 *Petrushka and the Dancer*, 198 (26 November 1935).
70 *Jack to Frances I*, 129 (Jack to Frances, letter 120, 14 September 1921).
71 *Petrushka and the Dancer*, 100 (Diary 12 March 1932)
72 *Petrushka and the Dancer*, 13 (13 August 1929).
73 *JCP/DMR*, 19 (JCP 3, 22 September 1929].
74 *JCP/DMR*, 34 (JCP 8, 15 September 1930).
75 DMR told her sister-in-law, Rose Isserlis Odle: 'It was our mutual dislike of the sex-as-a-whole that first drew Alan and me together.' Letter of 27 November 1949, in *Windows on Modernism: Selected Letters of Dorothy Richardson*, ed. Gloria G. Fromm (Athens & London: University of Georgia Press, 1995), 621.
76 *JCP/DMR*, 66 (JCP 23, 6 September 1932).
77 *JCP/DMR*, 20 (JCP 3, 22 September 1929).
78 *JCP/DMR*, 148 (JCP 53, 27 October 1938).

FLORENCE MARIE-LAVERROU

Dancing, after her fashion: John Cowper Powys and Isadora Duncan

After My Fashion was completed by 1920, though it was not published until 1980. Its belated appearance has meant that it has not yet been assimilated into the canon of John Cowper Powys's novels. In fact, it has over the past thirty years received very little critical attention at all, and the Picador edition of 1980 has never been reprinted. While this essay will not be arguing that *After My Fashion* is one of Powys's great novels, it will draw attention to its context within modern culture and modernist thinking, and suggest that a sustained analysis would be rewarding.

Readers with a biographical bent should be interested in Powys's only novel with an American setting; according to Morine Krissdóttir, his 'descriptions of the life in Greenwich Village are marvellous, culled directly from his own existence in New York ....' (Krissdóttir, 165) The plot itself can easily be related to Powys's life since the hero of the novel, Richard Storm, is an English poet with literary ambitions. His main rival, Robert Canyot, is a painter. Richard is also involved in an extra-marital love affair with a dancer, Elise. This is no mere chorus girl but a famous dancer able to pass judgement on Richard's poetry and to discuss her own art. According to Francis Powys, the model for Elise was Isadora Duncan, whom Powys knew well.[1] The text is rich in clues confirming this: like Isadora Duncan, Elise is successful both in Paris and in New York. Elise is seen dancing 'against the familiar background of plain black curtains' (179)—referred to again as her 'inevitable black curtains' (270)—just as Isadora Duncan used to dance against dark-blue curtains. Elise's dancing is said to evoke 'Dionysian passion' (271) and Isadora Duncan, who read Nietzsche's work,[2] once said: 'Dancing is the Dionysian ecstasy which carries away all.'

(Franco, 17) Moreover Elise is connected with revolutionary Russia when she falls in love with a young Russian with communist ideas, as was Isadora Duncan, who (apparently *after* the composition of Powys's novel) was to fall in love with the Russian poet Sergei Esenin and, in 1922, move to the USSR.

These biographical details, however interesting they may be in themselves, are not just anecdotal. They help the reader put into perspective some of Elise's comments on her art, for these can be compared with the writings and speeches of Isadora Duncan and with some critics' comments on her and on modern dance. Above all, they throw light on a quite unexplored dimension of the text—its theoretical dimension. C. A. Coates asserts that 'art is the real subject of the novel'; three of the main characters are artists; their conversations revolve around their artistic beliefs and stances (Coates, 23). These artists neither work nor speak in a vacuum. The text makes it clear that, having spent several years in France, Richard Storm is well aware of the new artistic experiments carried out on the Continent: 'I think we're bound to take a critical interest in every new experiment.' (43) Powys wrote his novel after the First World War at a time when those who were to become the great modernist poets and novelists had started to voice their opinions about art. It should be no surprise, then, that their theories, which on the whole, aimed to break away from realism and representational writing and painting, are hinted at in a work whose subject is art and whose main protagonists are intelligent and articulate artists speaking for poetry, painting and dancing. These three art-forms were closely connected and underwent major changes in the first two decades of the twentieth century. Leaving aside for now the conversations between Richard Storm, the poet, and Robert Canyot, the painter, I will focus on those between the poet and the dancer.

In this context we need to recall the crucial role that the art of dance played at that time in the elaboration and expression of a new aesthetic. Often referred to as the topos of the Dancer, this aesthetic is exemplified by Diaghilev's Ballets Russes and by Gaudier-Brzeska's sculpture 'The Dancer' of 1913. Even before the end of the nineteenth century and the dawn of the modern period, the French poet Stéphane

Mallarmé had considered the art of dance to be a metaphor for the art of writing; he viewed dance as defying the separation between form and content, the dancer being 'the emblem of identical form and meaning' (Kermode, 71). Other writers and poets (Paul Valery, Arthur Symons, W. B. Yeats) thought along these lines and elaborated on this metaphor in order to define the new aesthetic. In *Romantic Image*, Frank Kermode contends that in their rejection of Cartesian dichotomies (body and soul; action and passivity; form and meaning; subject and object) and in their attempts to go beyond discursive language and mechanical patterns, many poets and writers came to consider the image of a woman's body in movement—and more precisely the image of the dancer—as exemplifying what they meant by the aesthetic image: the poem 'has meaning only in terms of its expressive body, like a dancer.' (Kermode, 56)

We will move from an analysis of Elise and Richard's artistic conversations and of Elise's performances in so far as they pertain to some aspects of the aesthetic debates of the time (in particular the ideas of impersonality and emotion, and the link with tradition) to a more elaborate reflection on the arts of dancing and writing in a modernist context. We need to understand better the extent to which the image of the dancer in *After My Fashion* reveals the desire of modernist writers to discard representationalism. With that work done we can then open new vistas through the optic of the French philosopher Jacques Derrida, whose ideas on the art of dance are related to a new ethics.

The second part of *After My Fashion*, which begins with Chapter Thirteen, takes place in New York. It is there that (in Chapter Fourteen) Richard meets Elise again, two months after his arrival in North America. She had been his lover in Paris, but it is above all as a 'great dancer' that Richard chooses to value her. (179) Since he has had difficulty in getting accustomed to his new life in New York and to its urban landscape, Richard is not only thrilled but also simply relieved to see her again: 'his spirit rose up, healed and refreshed, to greet her' (179). In fact the art of Elise soothes him because the rhythm of her dancing is different from the rhythm of New York. In that sense it enables him to rediscover the rhythm of the world and the beat of Nature which, in Richard's opinion, is no longer to be felt in New York: 'she lifted for him the veil of Isis' (179).

The reference to the goddess, the patron of nature and magic and the archetype for creation, clearly hints at Isadora Duncan herself, who once wrote: 'I am called Isadora—That means Child of Isis—or Gift of Isis.' (Duncan, 21) It is also an indication of the status of Elise's art and her will to discover and be in harmony with what 'lies behind all this cause and effect' which characterizes the modern world (195). In other words, modern dance discloses what lies behind a purely metonymic and mechanical order of the universe, as embodied in New York. Her vision of the world thus seems, at first, to be akin to Richard's and to parallel that of the Romantics whose stance and poetry stressed the links between humanity and the cosmos. Romanticism was invoked to resist those impersonal forces that were felt to be damaging and even destroying the harmony between humanity and Nature: 'This was what he had been aiming at in his own blundering way; this was what he was born to understand! The softness of ancient lawns under immemorial trees, the passion of great winds in lonely places, the washing of sea-tides under melancholic harbour walls.' (180) The first visions that Richard sees in his mind's eye when watching Elise's performance are recollected sounds and images of the natural world ('lawns', 'trees', 'winds', 'sea-tides'), which come as a relief to him in the iron-made space of New York. Elise seems to be able to conjure up both the eternal universe and the natural world through the spiritual movement of her body, a movement which is in turn inspired by the movements of the world. This was the case for Isadora Duncan who aspired to realize in dance 'a movement which … sets itself in harmony with the motion of the universe.' (Duncan, 33) These connections are not only modern; they are also archaic: 'There was about it something of that kind of ritualistic imagination which, perhaps erroneously, the modern has come to name "archaic".' (270) In this respect, modern dance and the modernist (or post-Romantic) aesthetic can be said to reach for the impersonal, for a primordial sense of being, before the emergence of subjectivity and personality.

Contrary to Richard's initial feeling of responsiveness and accord,

Elise's art actually refutes and contradicts his ideas, and shows him the limits of his aesthetic solutions: his solitary romantic cultivation of the subject is challenged by her pursuit of the impersonal as a means of responding to the universal and the cosmic. In the course of conversations between Elise and Richard some words and terms are recurrent. Richard considers that the aim of art is to express 'the merest personal sensation of one individual' (220), and this is precisely what Elise reproaches him with, telling him that his poetry is 'the expression of a good deal in you that is merely personal. It is too self-satisfied ... .' (221) The dancer, by contrast, practises an art that conveys 'an emotion that expresses the only really impersonal thing in the world' (220). Since *After My Fashion* was being written in 1919, the reader can link it chronologically to one of the main tenets of modernism, articulated by T. S. Eliot in 1919. His essay 'Tradition and the Individual Talent' affirms that the 'progress of an artist is a continual self-sacrifice, a continual extinction of personality' (Eliot, 17), and that 'Poetry is not a turning loose of emotions, but an escape from emotion; it is not the expression of personality, but an escape from personality.' (Eliot,19) In the same vein, in 1920, while commenting on the difficulty of achieving impersonality, Virginia Woolf found fault with the writings of both James Joyce and Dorothy Richardson precisely on those grounds: 'the danger is the damned egotistical self, which ruins Joyce and Richardson' (Radford, 88). Both Eliot and Woolf, with other writers such as Katherine Mansfield, considered that what was personal was bound to be narcissistic and was doomed to fail from an aesthetic point of view. The aim of those writers was to go beyond the age-old lyrical voice of feeling and desire, beyond both the subjective visions of the Romantics and the sentimentality of the Victorians, so as to create a new aesthetic: this would be labelled modernism.

In *After My Fashion* Elise criticizes Richard's work by comparing it with that of the Romantic poets: 'You don't mean to say you think you have rivalled Shelley and Keats in these verses? They are very beautiful and right, those old poets, but you can't do that sort of thing twice. You've got to go further. You've got to start where they left off. You've got to say something new.' (220) The anaphoric 'You've got to' stresses the urgency of the task which lies ahead for Richard, a task imposed on him from the outside, by the world, and by history, in the person of Elise.

Although 'impersonality' is the key term of contention in the debate between Elise and Richard, the dancer allows that impersonality does not exclude emotion altogether: 'It's an emotion …' Elise says of the drive to impersonality (220). Thus we are presented with one of the contradictions at the heart of modernism. Modernism has often been associated with formalism, and a rejection of sentimentality, though emphasis is occasionally laid on its emotional qualities: 'the importance of feeling, emotion and introspection in modernist writings, which links them to the Romantics and the theory of sensibility, has been acknowledged by some critics.' (Ganteau & Reynier, 12) In order to reconcile these two views it has been argued that, contrary to his explicit claims, the real achievement of T. S. Eliot was to articulate and harmonize the contrary notions of impersonality and emotion: 'Impersonality, for Eliot, is the condition for the creation of an "impersonal" emotion—"significant emotion"—emotion which has its life in the poem and not in the history of the poet.' (Reynier, 300) In much the same way, the realization of 'de-subjectified emotion', one of the aims of the modernist writers, was also at the core of modern dance in general: 'a defamiliarization of bodily emotion through the primitive, mechanical, or futuristic sources of movement innovation and the return of expression, once emotion is expunged, as a depersonalised ('universal') embodiment of subjectivity' (Franco, x-xi). Thus, it is fitting that Elise, whose character is drawn from Isadora Duncan, epitome of modern dance, should fight for universal subjectivism against personal subjectivity, and for depersonalised emotion against isolated lyrical emotions and sensations.[3]

By 'subjectivism', distinct from 'subjectivity', is meant a respect for the subjectivity of others, a resistance to seeing other subjects as objects, and an acknowledgement of the limits imposed by one's own subjectivity on any claim to objectivity. The relevance of this can be traced in the debate over the term 'Einfühlung' or 'empathy', given intellectual currency by the art historian Wilhelm Worringer in 1907, and a highly topical term in about 1919. Further development of Kant's subjectivism is adumbrated by the concept of the 'transpersonal', apparently coined by William James in 1905. Much of the advanced (post-Nietzschean) thinking of those years was aimed at undoing the categories of subject and object. Those categories are emblematically dissolved in the dancer, the creator at one with what is created, the performer inseparable from the performance: so W. B. Yeats, in 'Among School Children' (1926), celebrated that achieved dissolution: 'How can we tell the dancer from the dance?'

The debate between Richard and Elise carries conviction because it does not remain on a theoretical level. Richard is twice given the opportunity of admiring Elise's art of dance. On the first occasion, emotion is in the foreground, for Richard is clearly enthusiastic about meeting Elise again and he is overwhelmed by what he experiences (179–180). Yet, right from the start and before speaking to Elise, he realizes that the emotion which her dancing provokes has nothing to do with his usual sensations (180) and is opposed to egotistic effusion: 'But her dancing was not the wild lyrical outburst of an emotion that spurned restraint' (180), a sentence which echoes Eliot's 'Poetry is not a turning loose of emotion' (Eliot, 21). At the second of her performances (270–73), the impersonal dimension of Elise's art is highlighted. Her dancing shows Richard ways of being impersonal without sacrificing emotion altogether. The narrator, who has adopted Richard's point of view, insists that in her dancing depersonalisation has been achieved.

This impersonality or depersonalisation finds its roots in the relation of the performance with the past. The narrator says about the architecture of the new Stuyvesant Theater (where Elise dances) that 'the decoration was not only simple; it was austere. It was rigid and reserved in a manner that was suggestive of Byzantine work' (270); its architect is said to be 'some unknown boy out of the far west whose youthful receptiveness was that of a reed played upon by the undying spirit of dead generations' (271). As for Elise's dancing itself, it is compared to a 'ritual' and characterised as 'Dionysian'—two words which convey the past and confirm the parallel between Elise and Isadora Duncan. The ritual character of Duncan's dancing has been related to one of the aspects of Eliot's theory of impersonality in art. Eliot contended that the process of depersonalisation could be achieved through the poet's 'relation to the dead poets and artists' (Eliot, 17). This does not imply that the poet is to reproduce them in a servile way but that the poet 'must develop or procure the consciousness of the past.' (Eliot, 17) Isadora Duncan's emphasis on the ritualistic dimension of her performances, and on their links with an archaic practice, leads a recent critic to suggest that 'by sacrificing the expression of her personality to the reinterpretation of past art, Duncan is typically modernist in Eliot's sense.' (Franco, 18) One should stress that Elise's/Isadora's reinterpretation of dance had nothing to do with servile imitation. The relation was dynamic and designed so that the past and the future came together. This the narrator of *After My Fashion* is keen to underline in describing Elise's performance: 'there had been evoked something ... suggestive of the passion of the human spirit ransacking the remote past and steering into the unborn future.' (270) The sentence echoes some of Isadora Duncan's statements: 'While my dancing owes inspiration to the Greeks, it is not Greek really, but very modern' (Duncan, 51); 'I don't mean to copy [the chorus], to imitate it, but to be inspired by it, to recreate it in myself with personal inspiration; to take its beauty with me toward the future.' (Franco, 18) The depersonalisation of art cannot be achieved by imitation (as Richard tries to argue) but only through creative dialogue, the way of Elise.

Far from being the exclusive achievement of one particularly gifted dancer, Elise's performance is 'the resultant harmony' (271) of multiple influences and of multiple voices: 'The quiet cynical Roger, the inscrutable Ivan, his own ivory goddess had together produced something through the medium of an American boy of whose very name he was ignorant.' (271) The anonymity of the young architect who is said to be either a 'reed' or a 'medium'[4]—that is to say somebody who has managed to go beyond his or her personality; words such as 'together', 'melt into', 'harmony' (271); the recurrent use of the expression 'musical rhythm' to refer both to Elise's dancing and to the architecture of the theatre: everything points to 'the amazing *anonymity* of the whole thing' (271) that is to say, to the process of depersonalisation at work. Music, architecture, politics all contribute to Elise's performance. Her creation is obviously not the expression of one particular individual, nor of a single discipline. Art is the result of multiple voices or of a multi-faceted subject.[5] This is all the more obvious as the narrator suggests that such a conception of art makes room for the role of the audience: 'it seemed as though the youthful architect had allowed for the very audience there, and had given it also a part to play in the resultant harmony.' (270) Such a conception of style seems to be at odds with that of Richard who is content to express 'the merest personal sensation of one individual' (220), until he finally responds to Elise's dance and becomes aware of its potential: 'Richard felt ashamed of himself, of his own inadequate and chaotic work, in the presence of this achievement.' (271) The reader, however, is denied the opportunity to follow the influence of Elise's second performance on Richard's work, since Richard dies in the following chapter.

Elise's art of dance may be in the limelight and yet, as suggested by Coates, it is art as a whole which 'is the real subject of the novel' (Coates, 23). Elise's art points stylistically in directions that are immediately relevant to the modernist literary debate, directions that Powys was to follow in subsequent works.

As Mallarmé suggested, there are links that could be drawn between the art of dance and the art of writing, though one of the main differences between them must be the importance to dance of the incarnate body. It is through the body that the original rhythms of the world can be recaptured: the narrator speaks of Elise's 'arms', 'limbs', 'breasts', 'physical beauty' (180–81) and sums everything up by referring to her 'palpable presence' (270)—while mentioning Plato, which may be ironic. In that sense, the art of dance is prior to words and suggests an original, immediate and mute contact with the world. We must distinguish between language as expression and communication and language as pure sound, if we are to preserve the validity of Mallarmé's comparison between the two arts. (We might mention Gertrude Stein as an example of a writer whose language disdains personal expression and reaches for impersonality, even at the expense of meaning.)

Dancing has long been considered as a kind of language—'I use my body as a medium, just as the writer uses his words' (Duncan, 53)—as is intimated by the word 'choreography' and the fact that Terpsichore is one of the Muses. As a metaphor for writing, Mallarmé intends dance to do the spatial work of words distributed on the page, as in his most celebrated avant-garde poems. When the narrator of *After My Fashion* refers to Elise's 'movement', 'gesture' or 'the leap and the fall and the monumental balance of her divine white limbs' (180), he evokes a language, a bodily language. The difference between this bodily language and communicative language is that the dancer's gestures *create* the meaning, whereas communicative language is supposed to express or represent some meaning which already exists.

Elise's dancing does not imitate anything, and the time-worn dichotomy between what is imitated and what imitates must crumble since there is no chronological anteriority of the former over the latter. Elise's gestures are not merely signs, they are meaning itself as it appears on the stage and unfolds itself. This implies that meanings and signs cannot be distinguished. In that sense dancing does not mean anything: it is. And what it is cannot be expressed in any other way but only when the dancer dances, which is precisely the reason why, some years before Yeats, Stéphane Mallarmé considered the dancer as a metaphor for the poem. It is no wonder that the narrator asserts that Elise's art is 'an art that changed former values' (180). In fact the shattering of the theoretical dichotomy between words and meanings was precisely one of the aims of the modernist writers. They were wary of the traditional concept of language, and focused on the materiality of words, on their rhythms and sounds, to show that all these 'irrational' aspects also contribute to meaning. Words are not mere transparent signifiers; their density and substance as words participates in the impersonal emotions of literature,

> What it comes to in the end is that Pound, like Hulme, like Mallarmé and many others, wanted a theory of poetry based on the non-discursive *concetto*. In varying degrees they all obscurely wish that poetry could be written with something other than words, but since it can't, that words may be made to have the same sort of physical presence 'as a piece of string'. The resistance to words in their Image is explained by the fact that words are the means of a

> very different sort of communication; they are so used to being discursive that it is almost impossible to stop them discoursing. (Kermode, 136)

The narrator turns out to be incapable of summing up what happens on stage when Elise dances. There is no attempt to describe Elise's dancing because it cannot be paraphrased. There is something in dancing which exceeds communicative language in the same way as there is in poetry and literature. What dancing and literature also have in common, then, is that they deal with what is ungraspable. Thus, the narrator focuses not on Elise's dancing but on its effects on Richard, whose point of view the narrative adopts.[6] What matters is not to imitate another dancer's dance; the dancer herself does not try to imitate anything already existing in advance. Thanks to her trained body, she writes on a blank page, which is also the body itself following the rhythms of nature in a process, a performance which debunks the idea of mimesis.

Elise's choreography has nothing to do with a linear narrative or a metonymic structure. In contrast with walking, dancing could be said to be a 'practice of deviation', to use Michel de Certeau's phrase. Instead of going from one place to another, step by step, the dancer leaps and falls, she does not go anywhere in particular and she obeys metaphoric relations with no aim or purpose. Paul Valéry suggests the self-sufficiency of dancing: 'And in that world acts have no outward aim; there is no object to grasp, to attain, to repulse or run away from, no object which puts a precise end to an action and gives movement first an outward direction and co-ordination, then a clear and definite conclusion.' (Franco, 15) Modernist aesthetics tend to be metaphoric rather than metonymic.

Thus it transpires that what matters most is 'the rhythm of [Elise's] movements' (271), the 'musical rhythm' (270) of the performance as a whole, its 'harmony' (271), its sensuous form of emotion. One should keep in mind that the word 'rhythm' is probably derived from a verb meaning 'to flow' and refers to the never-ending and always changing flow of the deep. That is why the linguist Émile Benveniste suggests that rhythm is not to be thought of as a regular alternation of elements in a binary system, but as a movement which is susceptible to change at any time and in any direction, and which welcomes whatever is different and new (Benveniste, 333). In fact there seems to be nothing fixed in advance in Elise's dancing and when the narrator tells of the effect conveyed by her dance, the feeling one has is that it could go on and on, forever changing, forever transforming itself. This is supported by Richard's own 'interpretation'.

When Richard says: 'her spirit seemed to tear and rend at her beauty and mould it with a recreating fire into a sorrow, into a pity, into a passion' (180), the repetition of the preposition 'into' indicates that there is nothing chronological in this series. These emotions are simultaneous and yet they differ from one another. The same kind of comment could be made about the following sentence on account of its paratactic construction:

> this was what he was born to understand! The softness of ancient lawns under immemorial trees, the passion of great winds in lonely places, the washing of sea tides under melancholy harbour walls, the retreat of beaten armies, the uprising of multitudinous oppressed, the thunder of the wings of destroying angels, the 'still small voice' of the creative spirit brooding upon the foundations of new worlds. (180)

Richard's mind seems to be invaded by all these visions at the same time, even though the unfolding of the sentence could give the impression that they succeed one another. Everything exists both concomitantly and subsequently and there is nothing static in Elise's choreography. It changes continually: 'Elise danced a much larger variety of motifs than he had ever seen her bring together in one evening.' (272) It is forever transforming itself and never-ending: 'Thus he became more vividly conscious than ever of what he had always vaguely held; namely, that art is not something separate from life, but the premonition, reflected in human intelligence, of what nature is perpetually aiming at and never altogether reaching.' (271–72)

In all those senses, Elise's dancing can be seen as a form of stylistic experimentation enabling her to avoid stultifying conventions and to create a new aesthetic. This new aesthetic has much to do with the modernist one, based as it is on depersonalised emotion, metaphoric movements, the impersonal materiality that persists beyond any attempt to conceptualise or possess it, and the mediation between dialectical discontinuities: 'Richard noted that there was one insistent mood running through the whole series on that night, a mood that was at once heathen and Christian, rebellious and sensual, yet full of passionate faith.' (272)

The novel hints at the possibility of linking this new aesthetic to a new kind of relationship to the other, that is to say to a new kind of ethics. Before analysing this aspect, it is important to state that *After My Fashion* implies this possibility without actually showing it happening. This new ethic is shown by the way Richard's self-enclosed world is contrasted to Elise's opening onto the Other, as exemplified in her second performance. Elise's art is tantamount to a deposition of the ego, 'which is the very definition Levinas gives of ethics: "un incessant dégrisement du Même enivré de soi".'[7] (Reynier, 302) The remarkable recurrence of the word 'possessive', in describing Elise's second representation, points to this deposition of the ego:

> There was indeed something about this whole Christmas Eve performance that lifted him as it evidently lifted the girl by his side into a region where personal and possessive instincts had no place .... (270–71)

> some ritual that was itself a very dithyramb of exultant protest against all that was base, gross, possessive and reactionary amid the forces of the world. (271)

The adjective 'possessive' is related to the idea of what's personal, an idea Elise tries to reject.

The notion of 'possession' points to the influence of Nietzsche. In Nietzsche's writings, the words 'possession' and 'possessive' are constantly associated with the idea of sexual domination and sexual difference: 'what is at the core of all of Nietzsche's analyses of sexual difference ... are what might be called a process of *propriation* (appropriation, expropriation, taking, taking possession, gift and barter, mastery, servitude, etc.)'.[8] In other words, when the narrator suggests that Elise's art calls for the relinquishing of the notion of possession,[9] it could also be said that she is calling for a new relationship between the sexes. The theme is obviously important in *After My Fashion* with Richard torn between his wife and Elise.

That Elise's art of dancing can elicit the relinquishing of all possessive instincts is the outcome of what has already been noted: its perpetual movement, its everlasting rhythm and its constant displacement. Contrary to Richard's aesthetic practice, which is associated with the old world (233) and with the notion of imprisonment—'ancient barriers' (234)—Elise's choreography plays on constant movement and elaborates a new choreography of the self, which amounts to a new attitude towards others: we are even told, through Richard's eyes, that she dances to 'the music of every race' (272). In Derrida's terms, the characteristics of her dancing preclude all 'assigning of places' ('assignation à domicile'). 'The most innocent of dances would thwart the *assignation à résidence*, escape those residences under surveillance; the dance changes places and above all changes places.' (Derrida, 'Choreographies', 69)

Logically enough, this leads to a new way of envisaging sexual difference as revealed in the course of Elise's strange but intense dialogue with Ivan Karmakoff (252–3), the very structure of which is striking: it could be likened to a 'pas de deux' in which the two of them are so much engrossed that nothing else exists. The intensity of the encounter is rendered by the quick rhythm (keeping in mind Benveniste's explication) of the dialogue. What each character says is immediately answered by the other in a very smooth way: the two protagonists repeat and duplicate some words but also keep broaching new subjects without following any internal logic, and yet they appear to understand each other all the time. It is no wonder that they compare themselves to 'wild geese' discovering new spaces and new territories while looking down on the others, 'the seagulls' (253). Indeed Ivan Karmakoff refuses to view Elise as one thing or another: '"Do you like me better when I'm Greek or when I'm Christian?" … "You are never wholly either. You are a woman Dionysus."' (252) Elise cannot be classified and she cannot be arrested: she is neither one thing nor another; she is both and neither at the same time; she hovers and dances between the two. Ivan adds: 'Neither of us is pure woman or pure man. That's why we understand each other.' (253) All this may be purely theoretical; the relationship between the two characters is soon to peter out, but a similar impression of intensity and quality and liberty comes back the last time Elise is seen dancing on the stage. Her dance is the never-ending dance of sameness and difference, which amounts to the disruption of the hierarchies of binary oppositions. In other words, Elise's dancing would 'permit the invention of an other inscription, one very old and very new, a displacement of bodies and places that is quite different' (Derrida, 'Choreographies', 70). Her dancing becomes a metaphor for a continually evolving aesthetic operation liable to create new ethical relationships between the sexes. While Richard Storm searches for this through dance, that goal, however painful its attainment might be, is what drives the protagonist of each of Powys's novels.

Contrary to common assumptions, Powys was intensely aware of the literary, cultural and intellectual debates of his time. In this respect my argument supports that of Michael Holliday in *Making It New: John Cowper Powys and the Modernist Tradition* (2005). What I would stress is that the influence of modernism can be traced back to 1919–20. In *After My Fashion* Powys addresses central questions of modernism through the character of a dancer, that emblematic figure of the age. I would contend that Isadora Duncan's dancing, as presented in Elise's second performance, is one of the underlying influences on Powys's stylistic evolution from *Rodmoor* to *Weymouth Sands*; perhaps comparable in importance to the writings of Dorothy M. Richardson.[10]

After My Fashion remains, as a novel, traditionally within the realistic mode, demonstrating rather than enacting the issues it puts into play: the question of impersonality is a focus of interest which has not yet generated a radical approach to the writing of fiction. The text pays tribute to modern dance and endorses the avant-garde view that Isadora Duncan's achievement should be considered as an aesthetic breakthrough; yet from a stylistic point of view the novel remains unaffected by what it admiringly represents. What Powys learnt from Isadora would manifest itself in his later novels. A structural and tonal principle of 'depersonalisation' is evident in *Wolf Solent* and subsequent novels; this is realized through the use of multiple narrative voices, such as Bakhtin named polyphony.[11] In order to go beyond the traditional binary pairing that Elise/Isadora's dancing had so disrupted, Powys would rely increasingly on 'figural writing' and bring out the substantiveness of language, beyond the control or possession of any one speaker. By 1919 Isadora Duncan had, after her fashion, brought the dancer's art to unprecedented prominence; in the following decades that art would shape the novelist's.

NOTES

Numerals within parentheses in the text refer to pages in *After My Fashion* (1980).

1 'There can be no doubt but that Isadora Duncan is the model from which Elise the dancer in *After My Fashion* was drawn.' Francis Powys, Foreword to *After My Fashion*, p.5. In a letter to Dorothy Richardson, 16 October 1932, Powys speaks of Isadora Duncan as, apart from Richardson, 'the only other *great* feminine genius I've met & known at all (& her not as well as you though I saw her several times.)' (Fouli 70).

2 'And [Isadora Duncan] danced the Marseillaise for me once in New York. That was one day when I found her reading Nietzsche's *Birth [of] Tragedy*', John Cowper Powys quoted by Francis Powys, Foreword to *After My Fashion*, 5.

3 Such ideas, as we will see later on, had already been underlined by Stéphane Mallarmé when he spoke about Loie Fuller, who was Isadora Duncan's immediate forerunner: 'As Robert Greer Cohn notes of Mallarmé's writing on dance, its "joining function" is "that of the ritual whereby a crowd is joined to the all by an intermediary, that of the hymen between audience and nature with the impersonal dancer as go-between".' (Franco, 12) The word 'hymen' in this contexts derives from Derrida's *Of Grammatology*.

4 T. S. Eliot uses this very word in his essay, 'the mind of the mature poet [is] a more finely perfected *medium* in which special, or very varied, feelings are at liberty to enter into new combinations' (Eliot, 18, my emphasis); 'the poet has, not a "personality" to express, but a particular medium, which is only a medium and not a personality, in which impressions and experiences combine in peculiar and unexpected ways' (Eliot, 19–20, my emphasis).

5 '[G]uided by Nietzsche, [Isadora Duncan] turned to the choruses of Greek tragedy for inspiration. … Duncan decided that she would be the chorus, "I have never once danced a solo." … She wasn't so much choosing to play the one-who-stands-for

many as trying to suggest an entire dancing throng in which call and response become simply differing modes of a single plastic impulse … thereby giving the picture a heroic impersonality and magnifying herself into something more than a solitary woman dancing for an audience.' (Jowitt, 89)

6 Once again, we are reminded of Stéphane Mallarmé who did not want to describe the thing itself but the effect conveyed by the thing.

7 Emmanuel Levinas (1906-95): 'an endless sobering of the Same who is so drunk with the Self' (my translation).

8 'l'enjeu ou le ressort de toutes les analyses nietzschéennes sur la différence sexuelle … sur l'amour, l'érotisme, etc. ont toutes pour vecteur ce qu'on pourrait nommer le procès de *propriation* (appropriation, expropriation, prise, prise de possession, don et échange, maîtrise, servitude, etc).' Derrida, *Spurs* 108 / *Éperons* 109; English translation modified by author.

9 Isadora Duncan's dancing seems to have intimated the same idea: 'Isadora Duncan was a genius. She denied the right of private property in the dance.' (Michael Gold quoted in Franco, 6).

10 I have tried to demonstrate elsewhere that the extract from Christie's work in *Wolf Solent* can be read as a pastiche of Dorothy Richardson's style, without any mockery. What is at stake in this particular case is the question of feminine writing as it was formulated by Virginia Woolf and Dorothy Richardson. In fact the wider implications of the passage will be better understood if the extract is seen as an example of the conversation that was going on between Powys and Richardson. Furthermore, Christie's text invites the reader to go beyond any fixed position just as Elise's dancing does. See Florence Marie-Laverrou, 'John Cowper Powys dans le contexte moderniste: le hors-texte au cœur du texte', *Etudes britanniques contemporaines*, no. 30, juin 2006, 41–54.

11 See Charles Lock, 'Polyphonic Powys: Dostoevsky, Bakhtin, and *A Glastonbury Romance*', *University of Toronto Quarterly* 55, 1986, 261–81.

WORKS CITED

Benveniste, Émile, 'La notion de rythme dans son expression linguistique', *Problèmes de linguistique générale*, Tome I (Paris: Gallimard, 1966), 327–35.

Coates, C. A., *John Cowper Powys: In Search of a Landscape* (London: Macmillan, 1982).

Derrida, Jacques & Christie V. Macdonald, 'Choreographies', *Diacritics*, vol. 12:2, Summer 1982, 66–76.

Derrida, Jacques, trans. B. Harlow, *Spurs: Nietzsche's Styles / Éperons, Les styles de Nietzsche* (Chicago: University of Chicago Press, 1979).

Duncan, Isadora, *Isadora Speaks; Writings and Speeches of Isadora Duncan*, edited by Franklin Rosemont (Chicago: Charles Kerr, 1994).

Eliot, T. S., 'Tradition and the Individual Talent' (1919) in *Selected Essays* (London: Faber & Faber, 1951).

Franco, Mark, *Dancing Modernism, Performing Politics* (Bloomington: Indiana University Press, 1995).

Fouli, Janet (ed.), *Powys and Dorothy Richardson: The Letters of John Cowper Powys and Dorothy Richardson* (London: Cecil Woolf, 2008).

Ganteau, Jean-Michel & Christine Reynier, 'Introduction' in Reynier & Ganteau 11–16.
Holliday, Michael, *Making It New: John Cowper Powys and the Modernist Tradition* (London: Cecil Woolf, 2005).
Jowitt, Deborah, *Time and the Dancing Image* (Berkeley: University of California Press, 1988).
Kermode, Frank, *Romantic Image* (London: Routledge & Kegan Paul, 1961).
Krissdóttir, Morine, *Descents of Memory: The Life of John Cowper Powys* (London: Duckworth, 2007).
Lock, Charles, 'Polyphonic Powys: Dostoevsky, Bakhtin, and *A Glastonbury Romance*', *University of Toronto Quarterly* 55, 1986, 261–81.
Marie-Laverrou, Florence, 'John Cowper Powys dans le contexte moderniste: le hors-texte au cœur du texte', *Etudes britanniques contemporaines*, no. 30, juin 2006, 41–54.
Powys, Francis, Foreword to *After My Fashion* (London: Picador, 1980), 5–7.
Powys, John Cowper, *After My Fashion* (London: Picador, 1980).
Radford, Jean, 'Impersonality and the Damned Egotistical Self: Dorothy Richardson's Pilgrimage', in Reynier & Ganteau, 88–95.
Reynier Christine, 'Jeanette Winterson's Cogito – 'Amo Ergo Sum' – or Impersonality and Emotion Redefined', in Reynier & Ganteau, 299–308.
Reynier, Christine & Jean-Michel Ganteau (eds), *Impersonality and Emotion in Twentieth Century British Literature* (Montpellier: Presses de Université Paul Valéry, 2005).

Vera Wainwright in front of her Cottage Mockery Gap.
'Myself (not flattering!)'. © *April Parks* (*See article on page 144.*)

ANGELIKA REICHMANN

Dostoevsky in Wessex: John Cowper Powys after Bakhtin and Kristeva[1]

Introducing his analysis of John Cowper Powys's *Homer and the Aether*, Lock (2006) recalls how in the early 1980s Jeff Kwintner, proprietor of the Village Press, suggested to him that he should compare Powys with the Russian thinker Mikhail Bakhtin on the basis of their shared interest in Dostoevsky and Rabelais.[2] That story is strangely reminiscent of mine—or I should rather say, my story is an uncanny repetition of his: as an undergraduate student in Hungary, majoring in English and Russian, I followed a young professor's hint to read *A Glastonbury Romance* and made, in 1998, the same discovery as Professor Lock the moment I glanced at the list of Powys's works on the inside cover of the 1955 Macdonald edition. Consequently, as the topic of my doctoral dissertation I chose to make a comparative analysis of three novels: Dostoevsky's *Devils*, and two of its Modernist rewritings (as I thought then). One of these novels was Andrei Bely's *Petersburg*, the other was *A Glastonbury Romance.* However, the chapter about Powys never got written: pressed for time, as always, I gave up fighting with the immense complexity of the novel. It was only some years later that I read Professor Lock's groundbreaking study 'Polyphonic Powys' from 1996 and was more than happy to find that any chapter of mine would have been superfluous. His claims for the polyphonic quality of *A Glastonbury Romance*,[3] its direct relationship with Dostoevsky's *Devils*[4] and its similarly unreliable narration[5] reassured me that I had been thinking along the right lines; and they remain highly inspiring. His study convinced me that although there are numerous and quite obvious thematic parallels between the novels of Dostoevsky and Powys, there is much more fertile ground for further research in questions of narration, dialogue and the intertextual nature of the characters' narrative identities.

Thus, the present paper is a new beginning, the outline of a project for widening the scope of comparative analysis between Dostoevsky and Powys to include the four Wessex novels. This analysis will be conducted partly along Bakhtinian lines and partly by incorporating some aspects of psychoanalytic literary criticism—hence the title of the present paper, inspired by Malcolm V. Jones's most fascinating *Dostoevsky after Bakhtin*. I would like to examine four points of intersection between the Dostoevsky canon—that is, as formulated by Powys: Dostoevsky's four major novels and *Notes from the Underground*[6]—and Powys's 'Wessex novels': their approach to realism, the carnivalesque and its discourses, the intertextual nature of narrative identity, and the use of the confessional mode. Though space permits me to give here only summary references to each of the novels, my thinking about the four Powys texts is based on research that has led me already to publish articles on *Wolf Solent* and *Weymouth Sands*. It should also be acknowledged here that in talking of doubles and the miraculous I may appear to be staying close to the *themes* of the novels; it is important to recognize that, for great novelists, themes are also narrative devices: they are already and always doing double-duty, or doing duty as doubles.

Regarding their approaches to realism, both authors seem to disrupt realistic conventions to a certain extent, yet each has a distinctive mode of presenting the characteristic disturbances to the reality effect. In his book-length study, which is probably the most comprehensive post-Bakhtinian assessment of Dostoevskian realism, Jones uses the term 'fantastic realism' to characterise Dostoevskian texts. He emphasises that although the notion originates in Dostoevsky's own description of his art, it is a contested one:

> There is ... a difference in opinion between prominent Western critics about whether fantastic realism designates a higher spiritual or poetic reality and if so what kind of realm this is; whether, for instance, it is a higher religious realm in which the multivoicedness of human discourse (Bakhtin's heteroglossia) finds unity ...[7]

For his part, Jones insists that many characteristic features of Dostoevsky's texts connect his 'fantastic realism' to 'a modernist or post-modernist perception of the various ways in which discourse breaks loose from the reality principle and suffers internal fracture'.[8] Consequently, Jones defines 'fantastic realism' as a combination of three different discourses: those of 'authority' (the voice of the father or literary precursor, constantly questioned, undermined, even deconstructed), 'mystery' (uncanny effects, like the double, which seem to threaten structure and signification) and 'miracle' ('an ideal event whose realisation would be inconsistent with the reality effect').[9]

Though Powys's readings of Dostoevsky lack the sophistication of Bakhtin's, Powys clearly senses—and applauds—the Russian writer's disregard for realistic conventions, which he sees as a representation of 'real "reality"'.[10] His own literary practice, in turn, is also difficult to define in terms of its deviation from realism. The very title of *A Glastonbury Romance* is a disclaimer of verisimilitude and realism: it is a *romance* and therefore by definition less realistic than 'a novel'. Ian Hughes presents a similar argument to defend Powys from the charge of writing shapeless, formless, bad novels: he claims that his early works are not 'novels', but philosophic romances and that they should be interpreted as such.[11] Morine Krissdóttir has drawn a parallel between Powys's novels and magic realist texts, even hoping that Powys might yet prove to be accessible to readers familiar with Gabriel García Marquez.[12] Though a claim for Powys as a magic realist would be hardly tenable on the basis of his Wessex novels—since the miraculous is never represented as a natural phenomenon for the inhabitants of his fictional world[13]—the comparison clearly draws attention to the anomalies inherent even in Powys's most 'realistic' and novelistic works. As they are in Dostoevsky's, for of course the Russian novelist is an acknowledged precursor of Marquez and the other Latin American practitioners of magical realism.

This basic similarity calls for a closer analysis in Dostoevsky and Powys of the two discourses that undermine the reality effect in Jones's reading: the representation of the uncanny, and of the miraculous. The Freudian term of the uncanny has generated much critical debate and Jones applies the term in the knowledge of the several shades of meaning that it implies.[14] Not only is it associated from its very birth with the ever-changing concept of the double or Doppelgänger,[15] but also with the idea of the castration-complex—a phenomenon that has been fundamentally reinterpreted since, notably by Samuel Weber. For him the experience of the uncanny is inseparable from moments of castration in the epistemological sense of the word: moments, when not exactly *nothing* happens, but something happens which fundamentally undermines the subject's position by revealing the gap between the signifier and the signified and thereby shaking forever their trust in signification. It evokes a distrust in signification and representation, which can never be undone or dissolved, and therefore results in lasting epistemological and ontological insecurity.[16] Jones's emphasis on the discourse of the uncanny in Dostoevskian texts thus highlights both the sense of identity crisis and the feeling of epistemological and ontological uncertainty as their dominant features—aspects which appear in a much more tragic light in his fiction than in Powys's.

First, the uncanny doubling of characters: this appears in both authors' works, though in Powys's novels it is not such an explicitly and consistently applied structuring principle; the obviously hallucinatory double never seems, in Powys, to acquire corporeal reality. As Jones argues, the tensions that explicitly structure such shorter texts as Dostoevsky's *The Double*, a gothic story of rivalry between doubles ending in the main character's madness, seem ready to explode in all his major novels.[17] Similarly, a number of carnivalesque doubles can be identified in Powys's Wessex novels, but their narrative function is much less obvious than in Dostoevsky's. *Wolf Solent*, a novel focused on an identity crisis, seems to include an excess of doubles, among them Urquhart and Malakite as the surviving doubles of William Solent, the dead father, and the same father-figure and Redfern serve as potential or ghostly doubles for Wolf himself. In *A Glastonbury Romance* the most striking and obvious doubles are Sam Dekker and Owen Evans, but the phenomenon can be easily extended to include John Crow and Tom Barter on the one hand, and Finn Toller and Mad Bet on the other. Sylvanus and Jerry Cobbold of *Weymouth Sands* are probably the most traditionally carnivalesque of these pairs, loosely conforming to the types of the holy fool and the clown, respectively. In

Maiden Castle, Dud No-man and Urien Quirm also function in many ways as doubles, with the addition of the grotesque beast-carving as a shadow-figure to both. Though many of these characters feel that their identity and even sanity is threatened by the uncanny presence of a real or ghostly double, none of them reaches the stage bordering on psychosis such as we find in Dostoevsky's novels. No Powysian figures thus endanger their sanity as do Ivan Karamazov and Stavrogin. Both of these have their own devils as an embodiment or manifestation of an aspect of their own selves—most bewilderingly, of the side that they like to consider their 'rational' selves.

The second discourse that disrupts the reality effect is the miracle. This might be the only device (or theme) that could be effective as a counterbalance to the devastating influence of the uncanny. If the most disconcerting effect of the uncanny is the disclosing of the abyss between the signifier and the signified, the 'miracle' might imply just the opposite: to quote Jones again, 'a metaphysics of presence in which the transcendental signified finds a divine guarantee'.[18] And so, Jones writes, in Dostoevsky's novels 'the demand for miracle is ever present', even though it 'never happens'.[19] It is exactly this openness of the Russian writer's textual world towards a metaphysical reality that Powys celebrates in *Dostoievsky* as being close to his own view. He describes the Russian writer's world as a 'world of four dimensions', in which there is a '*crack* in the cause-and-effect logic that two and two make four'.[20] Nevertheless, Powys also clearly senses, as does Jones (and many other Dostoevsky critics), the tension between the different and divergent discourses in each novel: in Powys's own words, between Dostoevsky's 'personal faith and doubt'.[21]

Taking into consideration Powys's acknowledgement of a metaphysical bent, it is not surprising, even fitting, that—as distinct from the Dostoevskian *craving* for the miracle—in *A Glastonbury Romance* the miracle actually does happen, though it is not much craved by the one who witnesses it. Yet the miracle is not unequivocally so: its representation is always ambiguous. Far from resolving the Dostoevskian dilemma by a simplistic and oversimplifying miraculous stroke, Powys's representation of the miraculous in *A Glastonbury Romance* has a disconcerting effect akin to the uncanny. (These double disruptors are in serious rivalry!) The miracle is represented either as a subjective and therefore questionable and often incommunicable reality, or, if depicted as a fact, an element of objective reality, it is shown from several colliding or inconsistent perspectives, from which no single coherent account can be shaped. The most obvious examples of the representation of miracle as subjective reality are the contrasting depictions of John Crow's and Sam Dekker's visions. As C. A. Coates points out, the subjective intensity of the two intrusions of the metaphysical into the physical is similar; nevertheless, John Crow finds it as easy to reject the experience with a sweep of the hand as Sam Dekker finds it natural to embrace it.[22] In both cases, the miracle seems to resist representation as far as communication between the characters is concerned, or an agreement among readers: Sam Dekker's often absurd attempts to share his experience with the town-dwellers equally undermine the reader's belief in the significance of the event, or even its actuality.

To take another example, the representation of Geard's Mark's Court adventure with Merlin successfully balances on the thin edge between a dream or hallucination on the one hand, and a miraculous (or uncanny?) experience on the other. The most glaring example of the immediate discrediting of a factually represented miracle is Geard's resurrection of the dead boy, in which case the potential miracle is undermined by the possibility that the boy had only had an epileptic fit and was not dead at all. Quite disconcertingly, life seems to go on in Glastonbury, just as if *nothing* had happened—as if a potential new saviour with Christ-like powers had not appeared at all—until the reader starts to doubt whether anything has really happened at all. By his representations of the miraculous, Powys does not resolve the epistemological and ontological insecurities he diagnoses at the core of the Dostoevskian crisis. Instead, as Lock points out, he creates a polyphonic text in which the characters—and the reader—learn to live with these insecurities and ambiguities without losing their sanity, in a way that foreshadows postmodernist modes of writing, and reading.

The absence of the tragic in Powys's mature novels is, I should argue, inseparable from the second major topic of my analysis, the difference in the two authors' reading of the carnival. While both writers are fascinated by the carnivalesque, Powys's connection with the carnivalesque tradition is more direct (circus, burlesque, pageant, fairground, puppet-show) and his interpretations—both non-fictional and fictional—are incomparably more optimistic.[23] By contrast, Dostoevsky's sense of the carnivalesque is mediated through the classical and Renaissance traditions and 'the objective memory of the … genre',[24] rather than through direct experience; this has been a commonplace in Dostoevsky criticism since the publication in 1963 of the revised edition of Bakhtin's *Problems of Dostoevsky's Poetics*. A much more contested aspect of this idea is Bakhtin's optimistic and even apparently naive reading of the carnival as an unambiguously liberating source of rebirth.[25] Scepticism about this axiom of Bakhtin's has had far-reaching implications for the interpretation of the carnivalesque in Dostoevsky's works. Here I agree with Michael André Bernstein's insight, taken up and advanced by Borys Groys, to the effect that the carnivalesque as presented by Bakhtin can have sinister implications.[26] Bernstein argues that Dostoevsky's carnival is not bound by the traditional time limits of the festival, and therefore becomes 'a permanent inversion of all values' with 'lethal' and 'savage' consequences.[27] Drawing rather heavily on Julia Kristeva's *The Powers of Horror: An Essay on Abjection*, Bernstein goes on to claim that Dostoevsky's texts give a 'bitter' reading of carnival, for they represent it as the realm of the abject and abjection.[28] Though the differences between Kristeva's and Bernstein's application of the term (reflecting their attitude to Bakhtinian thought) could be the subject of a separate study, for the purposes of this paper let me cite Bernstein's redefinition of the Kristevan abject:

> [According to Kristeva] the abject [is] a universal psychological condition, a fissure in the relationship between consciousness and corporality that arises at the most elemental levels of human response to the facts of physical existence itself. … It undermines the conventional Freudian distinctions between conscious and unconscious. … Linked primordially to the body's excretions, the abject 'is something rejected from which one does not part,' a horror that violates 'identity, system, order.' For Kristeva 'The corpse, seen

> without God and outside science, is the utmost of abjection. It is death infecting life.' From my [Bernstein's] perspective, abjection is a social and dialogic category, and its expression is always governed by the mapping of prior literary and cultural models.[29]

The concern with the abject and abjection, as several commentators on Kristeva point out, is also directly related to the problems of representation and thus leads back to the mode of representation in Dostoevsky and Powys: the abject resists representation in the Symbolic (language). Consequently, abjection must be sublimated and thus it gives rise to 'mystical' and 'aesthetic' (that is, artistic) discourses according to Kristeva[30]—a comment that would deserve comparison with Jones's claim about the discourses of mystery and miracle disrupting reality in Dostoevsky's art. Remarkably, from the whole Dostoevsky canon Kristeva highlights the author's fascination with the abject in Powys's favourite novel, *Devils*.[31] It is indeed an apocalyptic text that glaringly demonstrates Bernstein's claim about the 'savage' nature of carnival run amok by ending not in a Saturnian Golden Age but in an epidemic, the burning down of the whole town, torrential, flood-like rains, a series of murders and ultimately the main character's suicide.

The contrast between the Dostoevskian 'bitter' representation of the carnival as the realm of abjection and Powys's interpretation of the phenomenon is striking. His all-embracing optimism about the phenomenon clearly manifests itself in his *Rabelais*, as far as his non-fiction is concerned. It shows obvious parallels with Bakhtin's book on Rabelais,[32] though Powys of course does not use the term carnival, let alone apply it to Dostoevsky's works. Powys also notes and highly appreciates some elements of Dostoevsky's fiction which are carnivalesque in the Bakhtinian sense. Thus, he mentions the 'Dionysian element' in the Russian writer's texts;[33] his belonging to a tradition that includes Shakespeare, Cervantes and Rabelais,[34] in other words, carnivalesque writers;[35] his (rarely emphasised) sense of humour, which, like carnivalesque laughter, tends 'to mock' even 'the Absolute';[36] and the presence in his novels of fools, both holy and unholy.

Quite consistently with his non-fiction, three of Powys's Wessex novels embody an optimistic reading of the carnivalesque both at the thematic level (in the characters' life-philosophy, in their representation, and in the setting and plot) and in the formulation of the narrative voice. Thus, the transformation of abjection into a Rabelaisian, optimistically carnivalesque approach to the human body and life (or death and dissolution, for that matter) is a central element in the life-philosophy of characters such as Wolf Solent, John Geard and Sylvanus Cobbold. Among Powys's characters there are numerous carnivalesque clowns and fools (whether holy or not), for example William and Wolf Solent, Geard, Sam Dekker and Jerry Cobbold. In all four Wessex novels the setting is described as a carnivalesque underworld. Scenes and events abound in carnivalesque contrasting pairs and their inversion, including the pairing of official celebrations and respectable or even sacred scenes with their carnivalesque opposites; Mat Dekker's dinner party and Mother Legge's tea party in *A Glastonbury Romance*; the christening of Tossie's twins in the church and the blasphemous christening of Nell Zoyland's son in Whitelake Cottage. Time is structured in some cases by the temporary inversion of the values that characterize carnivals, most notably in *A Glastonbury Romance* where Geard's one-year reign as mayor strikingly resembles the ephemeral power of the Carnival King—in fact, a fool—even though Powys gave up his original plan to start the story on April Fool's Day. For this reader, however, the most remarkable achievement of Powys's handling of the carnival is embodied not in such elements of 'external carnivalisation'[37] as mentioned above, but in the optimistically carnivaleque tone of the narrative voice as a particularly successful artistic discourse for the sublimation of the abject. This feature is probably most clearly present in the impersonal though humorous and indulgent narrative voice of *Weymouth Sands*—a novel concerned almost exclusively with the abject. *Maiden Castle* should be treated as an exception among the four Wessex novels as far as its approach to the carnivalesque is concerned. This bitterly ironic text seems to question Powys's earlier optimistic readings through the representation of the female body as abject and of Urien's obsession with the abject. This is a desire which by definition cannot be fulfilled, since it simultaneously attracts and repels.[38] The work of abjection is maddening, and disintegrating. Nevertheless, none of Powys's Wessex novels culminates in such an apocalyptic carnival as does Dostoevsky's *Devils*.

Apart from the thematic and narrational aspects of carnivalisation there is a third, equally important element of the carnivalesque tradition in both Dostoevsky's and Powys's texts: the representation of narrative identity. Relying on Lacan's ideas, Peter Brooks, an eminent advocate of psychoanalytical literary criticism, argues in *Reading for the Plot* that the 'question of identity ... can be thought only in narrative terms',[39] whereas 'it is in essence the desire to be heard, recognised, understood, which, never wholly satisfied or indeed satisfiable, continues to generate the desire to tell, the effort to enunciate a significant version of the life story in order to captivate a possible listener'.[40] Partly as a result of writing within the same carnivalesque tradition, both Dostoevsky and Powys disclose the intertextual nature of narrative identity; however, their reactions to a lack of originality, or a failure of identity, and the sense of belatedness that it implies, seem to be radically different.

Bernstein's reading of Dostoevsky is clearly informed not only by Harold Bloom's notion of the anxiety of influence[41] but also by René Girard's idea of 'mimetic rivalry', the doubling or imitative or mediated nature of novelistic desire.[42] And Bernstein convincingly argues that the typical Dostoevskian hero—from the Underground Man to Ivan Karamazov—can be defined by the term 'Abject Hero'. This is a particularly bitter version of the Saturnalian (carnivalesque) ironist who is outraged at his own belatedness, his lack of originality and his inability to break out from the already existing literary scenarios and motifs, even when he wants to define his identity through a narrative of his own.[43] As Bernstein emphasises, the major irony of the situation is that the 'Abject Hero' is bitterly conscious that 'even his most "personal" longings are only commonplace quotations';[44] in other words, his characteristic state of mind is what Nietzsche so magnificently condemned as *ressentiment*.[45] Bernstein focuses on the plight of the Underground Man and the clown figures in Dostoevsky's texts, but one of the best examples is Stavrogin's confession in *Devils*, which, instead of presenting an authentic narrative that would define Stavrogin's identity, is only a rewriting of the Marion scene from

Rousseau's *Confessions*. Thus even a 'true confession' can hide behind the mask of a literary stereotype.[46]

Powys's non-fiction suggests a similar consciousness of the intertextual quality of narrative identity, though without *ressentiment*: Powys had learnt at least that much from Nietzsche. Reading—especially 'the western canon'—plays for Powys a major role in the formulation of one's 'life-illusion' or personal philosophy.[47] What I would like to call attention to now is a specific aspect of his reading practice: he suggests that one should read literary works to enrich and enhance his or her sensations.[48] These sensually engineered experiences are clearly analogous to such favoured concepts of English Modernism as Virginia Woolf's 'moments of being' or the Joycean epiphany. This implies the reading of nature and the body through the Symbolic, through language and text: what is more, through already written literary texts. With some necessary simplification one can claim that Powys actually advocates the reading and narrative practices that cause the Dostoevskian hero's often catastrophic predicament.

Consistently with his non-fiction, Powys creates fictional characters who are quite content to see their own narrative identity as a compilation or metatext, created in a manner comparable to Modernist collage and foreshadowing the post-modernist attitude to already existing artefacts as raw material to play with. Thus, many of his major characters are not artist figures, not even obsessive talkers about themselves, but writers indulging themselves in literary and historical hackwork and producing no affirming narrative identity but quasi-historical compilations or unofficial, carnivalesque counter-histories, such as Wolf Solent's *Dorset History*, Owen Evans's *Vita Merlini* or Dud No-man's *Mary Channing*. The implied metatextual nature of these writings becomes obvious in the light of the weight given to *The Philosophy of Representation*, the metaphilosophical work undertaken by Richard Gaul in *Weymouth Sands*, or to the intricate inter- and meta-textual relationships between *Maiden Castle*, Hardy's *The Mayor of Casterbridge* and No-man's historical novel about Mary Channing.

This relatively playful approach to existing literary works as raw material does not at all hinder Powys from giving radical rewritings of his forerunners' texts (among them Dostoevsky's) at the thematic or ideological level. Examples of corrective rewriting include the internalisation of the carnivalesque clown as the father figure in *Wolf Solent,* instead of his murder in *The Brothers Karamazov;* the temporary realisation of utopia as a spiritual, artistic and political revival in *A Glastonbury Romance* instead of the disastrous fate of similar aspirations in *Devils.* Wolf Solent's carnivalesque, life-embracing personal philosophy—a philosophy Powys similarly advocates in his non-fiction—is the antithesis of Ivan Karamazov's narrative, which Powys reads in *Wolf Solent* and in *The Meaning of Culture* as an embodiment of defiance. The corrective addition here is the Nietzschean 'art of forgetting'[49] which is unattainable for Ivan Karamazov. In *A Glastonbury Romance,* however, Ivan Karamazov's argument about the rejection of God's world still returns as an important point to be criticised by Dr Fell.[50] Probably the most problematic and therefore often ignored rewriting is that of the character Stavrogin in Owen Evans; this rewriting involves, I would suggest, an act of self-purgation on Powys's part. As the quantity of examples also suggests, this zest for directly rewriting Dostoevskian themes apparently culminates in *A Glastonbury Romance*, after which direct references to the Russian writer disappear from the Wessex novels. One is of course still tempted in *Maiden Castle* to read the narratorial references to a 'chronicle' and the narrator's self-description as a 'chronicler' in terms of Dostoevskian allusion.

These differing attitudes to the intertextual nature of narrative identity are clearly responsible for a major difference in the structure of the two writers' texts. Given the polyphonic nature of their novels, we might expect a similar use of such discursive genres as dialogue and confession. In the case of Dostoevsky's texts the 'genre memory' of the Saturnalian dialogue and the penchant of the Abject Hero for 'self-laceration'[51] as a definition of his identity seem to lead almost inevitably to a preference for dialogue and the confessional mode. Among others, both Bernstein[52] and Brooks[53] point out how the (often abject) confession is a dominant element in Dostoevskian texts. It is so even if in many cases 'there appears to be no endpoint for confession other that that "motive for unmasking itself," which has no truth value.' As

Brooks argues, once 'faith and grace' become highly problematic concepts, as they do in Dostoevsky's novels, the 'confessional discourse' might turn out to be sterile,[54] as in the case of the Underground Man or Stavrogin. Though Dostoevskian confessions are often registered by the reader as less than heroic failures to create one's own narrative identity, his novels seem to insist on the necessity of confessional discourse. In Powys's Wessex novels, however, the opposite seems to be true.

In his non-fiction Powys clearly recognises the implications of the predominance of the confessional mode in Dostoevsky's writing: in a manner foreshadowing Paul de Man in *Allegories of Reading*[55] he connects the theatricality, the shameless exhibitionism and narcissism inherent in the confession with the autoerotic pleasure of solitary generation, that is, of the text.[56] However, while he applauds Dostoevsky's novels as the *author's* direct confessions, he is much more reserved on the *characters'* confessions, as is revealed by his remark on the '*abnormally* pronounced emphasis on talk'.[57] The full implications of this reservation can probably be best assessed in the context of Powys's rather misanthropic comments on verbal human communication—with special emphasis on unexacted or voluntary confession—as a waste of time, an offence and disturbance to one's immersion in sensations and the cultivation of his or her personal philosophy.[58] Powys seems to be turning a blind eye to the fact that it is Dostoevsky's characters who indulge in confessions. Thereby they are attempting to achieve an independent subject position, as Bakhtin convincingly shows.[59]

This 'blindness' is matched by the 'insight' to which the Wessex novels testify: they realise a more sophisticated critique of the confessional mode in Dostoevsky's texts than does any of Powys's explicit literary criticism. In fact, in *A Glastonbury Romance* this critique is formulated indirectly by a character. It is Lady Rachel whose thoughts imply a distrust in confessions, more particularly, confessions as they are represented in 'Russian stories'—presumably by, among others, Dostoevsky: 'Wouldn't it be like one of those reckless girls in Russian stories who pour out their burning heart-secrets at a touch, at a sign, at a glance?'[60] If, as Lock convincingly shows, Bakhtin really held speech in deep distrust,[61] Powys seems to share his suspicion: his representations of the confessional discourse reveal his distrust of oral communication as a means of achieving authentic subjecthood. His scenes involve depictions of the impossibility of full confession, indications that a confession has taken place without the actual representation of the moment and representations of the confessional situation of psychoanalysis (the heir to sacramental confession),[62] as vivisection.

The Wessex novels abound in examples of the impossibility of sharing one's inmost self—one's narrative identity—with another human being. Wolf Solent stops himself just before starting to reveal his 'mythology' to Christie Malakite. Sam Dekker is unable to interest his listeners in the story of his Grail vision: the only significant story of his life he has been willing to share, the story that, even if he has lost Nell, seems to define him for the rest of his life. As for the second case, the confession implied by a conspicuous gap in the text, *A Glastonbury Romance* provides the best example. Owen Evans's confession of his 'unpardonable sin' probably does take place—at least this is implied by the fact that Cordelia and Evans rush to the scene of the murder together—but if it is so, that cannot explain why it is omitted from the narrative of the novel. The third case is specific to *Weymouth Sands* whose most sustained metaphor for the 'talking cure'—the confessional mode in psychoanalysis—is vivisection. Finally, No-man's representation in *Maiden Castle* amounts to a satire on Powys's own exposition of personal philosophy and life-illusion: immersed in his subjective reality, No-man is often simply deaf to another character's confessional narrative.

John Cowper Powys confessed, indeed claimed that he was deeply influenced by Dostoevsky. The question of *how* exactly their texts are related to each other continues to be challenging. I do not pretend to have disentangled the complexities of the issue. All I can hope is that, by indicating these four points of intersection, I can provide a frame of reference in which it might become easier to grasp and interpret the often subtle and elusive intertextual bonds between the two novelists. At least in the Wessex novels, even this brief comparison suggests that Dostoevsky is a major source of inspiration for Powys (aesthetic, intellectual, formal, linguistic) in much more intricate ways than we might assume from any of his explicit comments on Dostoevsky.

NOTES

1 The present article is a version of the talk given at the 2009 Powys Society Conference in Llangollen. Let me express my deepest gratitude to all the members of the Society for their warm welcome and immense encouragement, and especially to Jacqueline Peltier, Charles Lock, Tim Hyman, Louise de Bruin, Belinda Humfrey, Michael Kowalewski, David Gervais and Stephen Powys Marks.

2 Lock, 'Powys and the Aether', 11.

3 Lock, 'Polyphonic', 263.

4 Lock, 'Polyphonic', 271.

5 Lock, 'Polyphonic', 274.

6 Cf. JCP's insistence on reading 'the four novels *as one novel*' and his Dostoevsky canon: John Cowper Powys, *Dostoievsky,* 42, 79. Here and in the rest of the article italics appear as in the original, unless indicated otherwise.

7 Jones, 3.

8 Jones, 28.

9 Jones, 191–9.

10 Powys, *Dostoievsky,* 19.

11 Hughes, 37.

12 Krissdóttir, 390–91.

13 This definition of magic realism is one of the most widespread and most easily accessible, as Tamás Bényei illustrates in the theoretical introduction of his monograph on the genre: Bényei 53–4. Nevertheless, the 'current critical consensus' about magic realism also involves the view that it is a fundamentally 'post-modernist mode of writing': Bényei, 15.

14 Freud's 'Unheimlich' rests on the notion of the return of the repressed, explained in his seminal essay entitled 'The Uncanny': '[If] every affect belonging to an emotional impulse, whatever its kind, is transformed, if it is repressed, into anxiety, then among instances of frightening things there must be one class in which the frightening element can be shown to be something repressed which *recurs.* This class of frightening things would then constitute the uncanny; and it must be a matter of indifference whether what is uncanny was itself originally frightening or whether it carried some *other* affect ... this uncanny is in reality nothing new or alien, but something which is familiar and old-established in the mind and which has become alienated from it only through the process of repression .... [It is] something which ought to have remained hidden but has come to light.'

15 In the same essay Freud identifies the theme of the double as one of the most frequently occurring instances of the uncanny. He works with literary material and

recognises the great variety of the forms in which doubling—the 'dividing and interchanging of the self,' 'the repetition of the same character-traits', or some hidden mental connection between two characters—can occur in fiction. He adopts Otto Rank's theory and interprets the psychological phenomenon of the double as 'originally an insurance against the destruction of the ego, an "energetic denial of the power of death"', rooted in 'self-love'. Thus he associates its emergence with primary narcissism and points out that once this stage of development is over, the double 'becomes the uncanny harbinger of death'. The concept has been thoroughly reinterpreted in a Lacanian context: see Dolar.

16 Weber, 1111–12.

17 Jones, 198.

18 Jones, 3.

19 Jones, 199.

20 Powys, *Dostoievsky*, 19.

21 Powys, *Dostoievsky*, 131.

22 Coates, 105–13.

23 'Carnival itself ... is a *syncretic pageantry* of a ritualistic sort. As a form it is very complex and varied. ... Carnival has worked out an entire language of symbolic concretely sensuous forms. ... This language ... gave expression to a unified (but complex) carnival sense of the world, permeating all its forms. ... It cannot be translated in any full or adequate way into a verbal language, and much less into a language of abstract concepts, but ... it can be transposed into the language of literature. We are calling this transposition of carnival into the language of literature the carnivalisation of literature': Bakhtin, *Problems of Dostoevsky's Poetics*, 122.

24 Bakhtin, *Dostoevsky*, 121.

25 'The carnival sense of the world possesses a mighty life-creating and transforming power, an indestructible vitality': Bakhtin, *Dostoevsky*, 107.

26 For a summary of these arguments, see Emerson, 171–5.

27 Bernstein, 20.

28 Instead of the essayistic and diffuse description of the abject in Kristeva's *Powers of Horror* let me quote the following brief definition for the disambiguation of the term: 'Every social order defines itself as opposed to the non-signified, the non-structured. ... the marginalised segments and elements are under the laws of prohibition and taboo: the filthy, the disgusting, the dirty, the perverse, the heterogeneous. The term *abject* includes all these elements that are not fixed symbolically, which are hardly encodable and are menacing for culture. The abject is the most archaic experience of the subject, which is neither an object nor the subject, but already articulates separation by marking the future space of the subject in relation to the disgusting, to the heterogeneous, and to the terrifying. ... it threatens symbolic fixation and the formation of identity. The aspect of the abject most imminently and constantly threatening the subject is the very existence and feeling of the body: it is this uncontrollable structure full of streams and flows that language, the word, and discourse must totally cover so that the subject can feel her/himself a homogeneous monad': Kiss, 19–20 (my thanks to Nóra Séllei for this translation).

29 Bernstein, 28–9.

30 Kristeva, 7.

31 Kristeva, 18–20; Powys, *Dostoievsky*, 19–20.

32 Though JCP's treatment of the French writer, with special reference to such chapters as 'Rabelais as a Prophet', must be taken with certain reservations, his understanding of the Renaissance text, though far from being so academic, bears comparison with Bakhtin's interpretation. Powys identifies roughly nine major components of Rabelaisian philosophy, namely 'the ataraxia of the Stoics', parody, 'farcical and sardonic humour', 'considerate humanity and pity', 'shameless realism and gross bawdiness', a 'Christian element', a 'magical and *almost occult* hero-worship', 'endurance, enjoyment, and unlimited toleration' and 'a *metaphysical* element': John Cowper Powys, *Rabelais,* 368–9. It must be noted that Powys, totally independently from Bakhtin's train of thought, emphasises some of the poetic dimensions of Rabelais' works: parody, grotesque realism/materialism, sardonic humour and bawdiness/comic treatment of the excremental and sexual, carnivalesque laughter, tolerance/suspension of official hierarchy: Mikhail Bakhtin, *Rabelais and His World,* 12–15, 21–2; 18–24; 7–10, 21–7 and Bakhtin, *Dostoevsky,* 127–8, 141–2, 193–4. These are features which Bakhtin, on the one hand, brought into the foreground of analysis, and, on the other hand, used as points of reference for his concept of polyphony formulated in his interpretation of Dostoevsky's poetics: Bakhtin, *Dostoevsky,* 6–7, 127–8, 193. In Bakhtinian terms, Powys, expressing a distrust in science typical of mythologically-oriented Modernists, poses against the monological 'truth' of reason a dialogical or polyphonic vision of his Rabelaisian 'Multiverse': Powys, *Rabelais,* 370. On the one hand, Powys's personal Rabelaisian philosophy is formulated in opposition to a crudely scientific approach manifested in such horrors as vivisection; on the other hand, it results in a pluralistic vision of the world: G. Wilson Knight, 85.

Jacqueline Peltier in her comprehensive study comparing Powys's different interpretations of Rabelais, also emphasises that Bakhtin's and Powys's works were written approximately at the same time and that Powys would probably have been highly interested in the Russian critic's interpretation, finding in him a kindred spirit. Though she follows the developments of Powys's interpretation only in his essays and critical works, Peltier takes it for granted that Rabelais' extremely deep influence on Powys's personal philosophy also surfaces in his novels.

33 Powys, *Dostoievsky,* 74, 165.

34 Powys, *Dostoievsky,* 45.

35 Bakhtin, *Dostoevsky,* 128; Bakhtin, *Rabelais,* 11.

36 Powys, *Dostoievsky,* 30.

37 Bakhtin, *Dostoevsky,* 180, note 31.

38 Kristeva, 1.

39 Brooks, *Reading,* 33.

40 Brooks, *Reading,* 54.

41 Bernstein, 106.

42 Girard, 1–15.

43 Bernstein, 17–22.

44 Bernstein, 105.

45 Bernstein, 108.

46 On Stavrogin's use of Rousseau, see 'The Marion motif: the whisper of the precursor' in Jones, 149–63.

47 Powys, *The Meaning of Culture,* 24–44.

48 Powys, *The Meaning of Culture,* 34.

49 Powys, *Dostoievsky*, 85.
50 Powys, *A Glastonbury Romance*, 691.
51 Bernstein, 93.
52 Bernstein, 90.
53 Brooks, *Troubling Confessions*, 46–60.
54 Brooks, *Troubling Confessions*, 48–49.
55 de Man, 283–6.
56 Powys, *Dostoievsky*, 72–3.
57 Powys, *Dostoievsky*, 22, emphasis mine.
58 Powys, *The Meaning of Culture*, 122–7.
59 Bakhtin, *Dostoievsky*, 21–2.
60 Powys, *A Glastonbury Romance*, 420.
61 Lock, 'Double Voicing', 71.
62 Brooks, *Troubling Confessions*, 52.

WORKS CITED

Bakhtin, Mikhail, *Problems of Dostoevsky's Poetics*, ed. and trans. Caryl Emerson (Minneapolis: University of Minnesota Press, 1984).

——, *Rabelais and His World*, trans. Helene Iswolsky (Bloomington and Indianapolis: Indiana UP, 1984).

Bényei, Tamás, *Apokrif iratok: Mágikus realista regényekről* (Debrecen: Kossuth Egyetemi Kiadó, 1997).

Bernstein, M.A., *Bitter Carnival: Ressentiment and the Abject Hero* (Princeton: Princeton UP, 1992).

Bloom, Harold, *The Anxiety of Influence: A Theory of Poetry* (New York: Oxford UP, 1973).

Brooks, Peter, *Reading for the Plot: Design and Intention in Narrative* (Cambridge, Massachusetts: Harvard UP, 1984).

——, *Troubling Confessions: Speaking Guilt in Law and Literature* (Chicago and London: The University of Chicago Press, 2000).

Coates, C. A., *John Cowper Powys in Search of a Landscape* (London & Basingstoke: Macmillan, 1982).

de Man, Paul, *Allegories of Reading* (New Haven and London: Yale UP, 1979).

Dolar, Mladen. '"I Shall Be with You on Your Wedding Night": Lacan and the Uncanny' *October* 58 (Fall 1991): 5–23.

Dostoyevsky, F. M., *The Brothers Karamazov*, trans. Constance Garnett (London: Heinemann, 1912).

Dostoyevsky, Fyodor, *The Possessed*, trans. Constance Garnett (London: Heinemann, 1914).

Emerson, Caryl, *The First Hundred Years of Mikhail Bakhtin* (Princeton: Princeton UP 1997).

Freud, Sigmund, *The Uncanny*, trans. D. McClintock (Harmondsworth: Penguin, 2003).

Girard, René, *Deceit, Desire and the Novel: Self and Other in Literary Structure*, trans. Yvonne Freccero (Baltimore and London: Johns Hopkins UP, 1988).

Hughes, Ian, 'The Genre of John Cowper Powys's Major Novels' in *Rethinking Powys:*

Critical Essays on John Cowper Powys, ed. Jeremy Robinson (Kidderminster: Crescent Moon, 1999) 37–48.
Jones, Malcolm V., *Dostoevsky after Bakhtin: Readings in Dostoevsky's Fantastic Realism* (Cambridge: Cambridge UP, 1990).
Kiss, Attila Atilla, "Miből lesz a szubjektum?" Hódosy Annamária and Kiss Attila Atilla *Remix (*Szeged: Ictus 1996): 9–53.
Knight, G. Wilson, *The Saturnian Quest: John Cowper Powys: A Study of His Prose Works* (Sussex: Harvester, 1978).
Krissdóttir, Morine, *Descents of Memory: The Life of John Cowper Powys* (New York: Overlook Press, 2007).
Kristeva, Julia, *Powers of Horror: An Essay on Abjection*, trans. Leon S. Roudiez (New York: Columbia UP, 1982).
Lock, Charles, 'Polyphonic Powys: Dostoevsky, Bakhtin, and *A Glastonbury Romance*,' *University of Toronto Quarterly* 55.3 (1986): 261–81.
——, 'Double Voicing, Sharing Words: Bakhtin's Dialogism and the History of the Theory of Free Indirect Discourse', *The Novelness of Bakhtin: Perspectives and Possibilities*, ed. J. Bruhn & J. Lundquist (Copenhagen: Museum Tusculanum Press, 2001) 71–87.
——, 'Powys and the Aether: the Homeric Novels', *The Powys Journal* XVI (2006): 11–33.
Peltier, Jacqueline, 'François Rabelais and John Cowper Powys,' *la lettre powysienne* 7 (2004).
Powys, John Cowper, *A Glastonbury Romance* (1932) (London: Macdonald, 1955).
——, *Dostoievsky* (London: The Bodley Head, 1946).
——, *Maiden Castle* (1936), ed. Ian Hughes (Cardiff: University of Wales Press, 1990).
——, *Rabelais* (London: Bodley Head, 1948).
——, *The Meaning of Culture* (New York: Norton, 1929).
——, *Wolf Solent* (1929) (Harmondsworth: Penguin, 1964).
——, *Weymouth Sands* (1934) (Woodstock, NY: Overlook Press, 1999).
Reichmann, Angelika, 'From Remembering the "Name-of-the-Father" to "Forgetting the Unpleasant"—John Cowper Powys's *Wolf Solent*', *la lettre powysienne* 15 (2008): 20–34.
——, 'In Love with the Abject: John Cowper Powys's *Weymouth Sands*', *The Powys Journal* XIX (2009): 79–106.
——, 'Reading Wolf Solent Reading', *Eger Journal of English Studies* Vol. 4 (2004): 45–55.
——, '*The History of Dorset* – Writing as Reading in John Cowper Powys's *Wolf Solent*', *Romanian Journal of English Studies* 1 (2004): 304–13.
——, 'What Made Ivan Karamazov "Return the Ticket"?—John Cowper Powys's Rabelaisian Reading of *The Brothers Karamazov* in *Wolf Solent*', *Annales Instituti Slavici Universitatis Debreceniensis* XXXII (2003): 261–81.
Weber, Samuel, 'The Sideshow, or: Remarks on a Canny Moment,' *Modern Language Notes* 88.6 (1973): 1102–33.

T. F. POWYS

The Wood
A play in one Act

N.B. At first reading, it would be advisable to ignore the deletions (in grey strike-through). These become useful after subsequently reading the following Afterword, at the beginning of which will be found a list of abbreviations used.

CHARACTERS

JOHN OWLSWORTH, a keeper

CHARLEY OWLSWORTH, his son

MARY KEYNE, ~~Charley Owlsworth's betrothed~~ a young woman

~~MR NEVILLE, a poor priest~~

~~A VOICE (Evil)~~

A CHILD

COUNTRYMEN:

WILLIAM SPOKES

WALTER HINDS

~~JAMES~~ JOHN PUNCHIN

THOMAS HINKS

COUNTRYWOMEN:

MOTHER SPOKES

MOTHER HINDS

MOTHER PUNCHIN

MOTHER HINKS

~~ACT I~~ SCENE I

Scene: A wood. In the time of ~~the great~~ war.[1]

~~It is evening in early summer, every leaf is full of grace and beauty, every blade of grass expresses a gentle gladness, every flower speaks of the eternal divinity of Beauty. There is only one presence in this scene of loveliness that shows a sinister aspect. This~~

There is a tall dead tree. This tree is bent and twisted in shape. It has a bare gnarled trunk, at the top of which there are a few withered boughs. Upon the ~~withered~~ boughs at the top of the tree a ~~hawk~~ raven has built its nest. By the side of the ~~hawks ravens~~ nest and tied by a string to a twig is a boy's cap.

The tree appears as an evil thing in the ~~beautiful~~ wood.

Under the ~~green leaves of the other~~ trees a pheasant is walking. A rabbit runs by and nibbles the grass and hops merrily away.

At a short distance ~~away~~ from the dead tree there is a path that is used sometimes by workpeople, who wish—when they know the keeper is not near—to cross the wood—on their way to the village.

Enter ~~lovingly~~ Charley Owlsworth and Mary Keyne.

Mary Keyne is dressed in a ~~simple~~ white ~~country~~ frock, such as girls wear in rustic places when they walk out with their young men.

~~About Mary Keyne there breathes the divine goodness of innocence. She looks like a woodland flower whose heart is pure love.~~ Charley Owlsworth is a young countryman with an intelligent face and laughing eyes. His voice though not over loud has the earthy note of one who has always lived amongst wood creatures and heath flowers.

Charley Owlsworth is dressed in his best holiday clothes, he carries a bundle in his hand.

The two lovers walk up to the dead tree and look up at the ~~nest hawk's~~ nest.

MARY KEYNE

Did you really climb up the tree Charley?

CHARLEY OWLSWORTH

Of course I did, how else could my cap have got there?

---

1 See the last paragraph of the 'Afterword' concerning impractical stage directions.

MARY KEYNE

But Charley, there are no branches until you get quite up to the top.

CHARLEY OWLSWORTH (*proudly*)

Yes. It's the hardest tree in the wood to climb. ~~Dad~~ Father said he'd thrash me if I tried it;[2] but I've been meaning to get at the ~~hawks~~ raven's nest for years.

~~You know how Father hates hawks, and now that I've tied my cap there the hawk will never come back.~~

[*They sit down and hold hands under the tree. All is stillness and peace.*]

MARY ~~OWLSWORTH~~ KEYNE

Charley I will try to be a good maid to your father. ~~It was good of M[r] Neville to persuade him to allow me to live with you.~~

CHARLEY OWLSWORTH

You have lived with us now for two months dear.

MARY ~~OWLSWORTH~~ KEYNE(*seriously*)

Don't you think it would be best Charley for me to tell your father that you have gone to the war?

CHARLEY OWLSWORTH (*decidedly*)

No ~~dear~~ it would ~~break his heart~~ kill him if you did. Now that he has taught me all the secrets of the wood ~~lore~~ he thinks of me as more than a son. His one idea, the one idea that makes his life happy is that I should follow in his steps and become a keeper. ~~There are two things in the world that Father loves, the wood and his only son. He would die were either taken away from him. But you know dear how simple Father is, that~~ You have only to say that I am coming back soon for his mind to be quite set at rest.

He does not know how many days pass. His life is not divided into days but into rounds. ~~When he goes his rounds morning noon and Eve his mind will rest quite contentedly.~~ He regards all the ~~rest~~ people of the world as poachers. He even thought of you as a poacher until ~~M[r] Neville~~ I explained to him what you were. ~~And you know that at first he thought M[r] Neville was a poacher.~~

[2] A rare Powys semicolon.

MARY ~~OWLSWORTH~~ KEYNE

But Charley wouldn't it be best to tell the truth? Suppose anything were to happen?

[*Mary turns her face away and when she looks at Charley Owlsworth again her eyes are ~~moist~~ wet.*]

CHARLEY OWLSWORTH ~~*(very feelingly)*~~

For my sake don't tell him dear. He is easy to deceive, he hardly yet understands that Squire Crew is dead.

MARY KEYNE

All the people in the Village know that you are going, old Mother Punchin asked me if it were true this very morning, and Mother Hinks looked so evil at me, as though she wished you might never come home. Why do old women wish such horrible things?

~~CHARLEY OWLSWORTH~~

~~Mr Neville says it is because they hate life at its best and only love it at its worst.~~

~~MARY KEYNE~~

Old men are better than old women.

CHARLEY OWLSWORTH

Yes old men are better.

MARY KEYNE

But young men are best.

[*Charley Owlsworth draws Mary Keyne to him and kisses her rapturously.*]

CHARLEY OWLSWORTH

[*releasing her*] I want you to tell ~~Dad~~ Father that I have gone to Norfolk to buy pheasant eggs, Squire Crew used always to buy his eggs from Norfolk. You need only say that I have been sent this time because so many eggs in the last lot were bad.

~~Dear you must promise;~~[2] ~~you must promise by all that we hold most sacred, by our love to one another, by our first walk together along the heath road—~~

Do you remember our first walk in the wood?

MARY KEYNE

Oh yes I remember, it was the day you ~~first told~~ showed me ~~about~~ the

~~hawks~~ raven's nest and told me how[3] ~~how~~ you wanted to climb up only your father wouldn't let you.

Oh I do wish you weren't going ~~out to this dreadful war~~.
[*Mary Keyne holds Charley Owlsworth to her.* ~~*as though she fears to let him go*~~]

CHARLEY OWLSWORTH

You must ~~be a brave girl~~ mind Father, there will be plenty for you to do when I am gone, you will have ~~Dad~~ him to look to.

MARY KEYNE (*timorously*)

It was not that, I know there will be plenty for me to do to keep my mind from worrying—but just now after I said how well I remembered that first walk of ours I thought I heard ~~a voice raven~~ the tree speaking. ~~amongst the leaves of the trees. The leaves rustled a little, did you notice?~~

CHARLEY OWLSWORTH

It was only your fancy, ~~the leaves~~ dead boughs often make queer sounds. They make queer sounds when they move, and when they are still they don't seem to ~~dreaming~~ rest.

MARY KEYNE

But these were real words, ~~they burnt into my heart. Oh~~ I can hear them now. ~~[*the leaves rustle and a strange voice that suggests the supernatural comes from the wood*]~~

~~THE VOICE~~

~~Keeper Owlsworth will know the truth when the rooks nest falls.~~

CHARLEY OWLSWORTH

[*who looks about him a little disturbed but answers happily enough*] I heard nothing. It's only your fear that puts funny thoughts into your head.

MARY KEYNE

Will the tree ever fall?

CHARLEY OWLSWORTH

Oh you needn't be afraid, I don't intend to climb the tree again, and if you want my cap so very much you must chop it down.

---

3 *told me how* is an editorial addition.

MARY KEYNE

Must I? Charley ~~is~~ be it easy to chop down a tree?

CHARLEY OWLSWORTH

You are more likely to kill yourself chopping down the tree than I was in climbing it. [*He looks upwards.*] The tree has stood many a ~~winter's~~ gale, and though it looks dead there may be sap in it ~~now~~. And even though the new Squire is ~~reputed to be~~ a mean hard man, he would hardly ~~dare~~ care to cut down this wood. ~~even in war time.~~

MARY ~~OWLSWORTH~~ KEYNE

[*kissing him*] Don't go dear. ~~, don't go, I feel as if some evil were coming upon us.~~

CHARLEY OWLSWORTH

Never fear for me, I shan't be gone long, they say that the war will be over by Christmas, and I'll be back to hear old Punchin ring out the old year, that is, if old Punchin isn't rung out himself first.

MARY ~~OWLSWORTH~~ KEYNE

Old folks live long in Enmore.

CHARLEY OWLSWORTH

But we young folks will live the longest. ~~[*The leaves rustle again but no voice is heard.*]~~ [*The boughs grate together.*]

MARY ~~OWLSWORTH~~ KEYNE

[*looks fearfully around.*] Did you hear anything?

CHARLEY OWLSWORTH

Of course there's nothing to hear unless it were the steps of the old work folk going by.
~~[*Seriously*] Mary~~ I must soon be off Mary. You shall have all the money I can get to you and ~~the new~~ Squire ~~Mr~~ Robinson has given ~~Dad~~ Father leave to stay in the old house and to walk his old rounds. ~~although Mr Robinson is no sportsman and has no use for a keeper.~~
~~[*hopefully*] I am glad Mr Neville has come to live in Enmore.~~

MARY KEYNE

How still and quiet everything is ~~now~~, I can't believe I heard any ~~ugly~~ nasty thing. ~~speaking. As soon as you spoke of Mr Neville the whole~~

~~wood seemed to become quiet.~~

~~And yet Mr Neville is such a queer old man.~~

~~CHARLEY OWLSWORTH~~

~~[*laughing merrily*] Oh dear Mr Neville is enough to make one laugh. Winter and Summer he wears the old black coat that you once[4] Only holes, there wasn't one pocket that hadn't a large hole in the bottom.~~

~~MARY KEYNE~~

~~What did he Mr Neville say when you searched him?~~

~~CHARLEY OWLSWORTH~~

~~Oh he spent the time in explaining to Father that the book he carried in his hand wasn't a partridge.~~

~~MARY KEANE~~

~~Mr Neville's a good friend to have though his coat's so old.~~

~~CHARLEY OWLSWORTH~~

~~Father would never have let you live with us unless Mr Neville had begged him to. Mr Neville managed to get Father to remember the days of his own boyhood, and Father spoke of Mother and of how he had sat with her many a time in the wood and walked out on the heath. And then Dad said you could come and live with us if you'd be a good maid and work.~~

~~MARY KEYNE~~

~~He doesn't think I'm a poacher now.~~

CHARLEY OWLSWORTH

~~No he loves you too—and dear~~ The time will soon pass, when ~~you~~ I come back ~~from my first leave, we will be married,~~ we will marry then.

MARY KEYNE

~~A Christmas wedding~~ Oh I shall love that.

CHARLEY OWLSWORTH

~~Let's make our ~~wedding~~ future plans.~~

[*Charley Owlsworth and Mary Keyne sit lovingly and talk in low voices.*

4 Something seems to be missing between the end of Ams p.18 and the beginning of Ams p.19. Perhaps a leaf or leaves have been torn or cut out—see notes 14 and 19 below.

Enter four old countrymen in working clothes coming from the fields. They are crossing the wood because they know that it is the shortest way to their homes. They know also that Keeper Owlsworth goes to bed early. The countrymen carry their empty food baskets and each man also carries a dead piece of wood.

They walk slowly as though they are tired. The foremost of the countrymen as he passes by the tree—though at some little distance therefrom—sees the lovers. He stops, and the other three following his example stop too.

The four countrymen stand very still as though they had become a part of the wood. They regard the pair beside the tree with a quizzical interest.]

JOHN PUNCHIN

'Tis Mary Keyne.

THOMAS HINKS

No thik bain't maid's name now, she be some'at else.

WILLIAM SPOKES

'Tis Mary ~~Owlsworth~~ Keyne.

WALTER HINDS

'Tis Mary Keyne. ~~that used to be.~~

JOHN PUNCHIN

Thee be right enough Walt, thee do truthfully tell it, for Mary do bide at Keeper's, an' 'tis Mary Keyne.

WILLIAM SPOKES

[*looking up at the tree*] Mary Keyne be Keeper's daughter.

THOMAS HINKS

Charley Owlsworth do go out wi' she.

JOHN PUNCHIN

'Tis 'e that be under tree.

THOMAS HINKS

I do mind Charley, 'e fought me boy Tom for thik maid on green years ago. Me boy Tom didn't do nothing to she except push she into pond, and in same pond 'e soon found 'is woon self pushed there by Charley.

WALTER HINDS

'Tis a deep pond.

THOMAS HINKS

So me boy said.

WILLIAM SPOKES

I do mind further back than Charley, I do mind when Keeper 'is self were married. Keeper were oldish then and she were Bill Bower's girl that were always the first to find they buttercups in May.[5]

THOMAS HINKS

'Twere a nice maid.

WALTER HINDS

So 't were.

WILLIAM SPOKES

[*looking up at the dead tree*] Tree be dead.

JOHN PUNCHIN

There be ~~leaves on~~ life in all the trees save thik woon alone.

THOMAS HINKS

'Tis true what John do say.

WALTER HINDS

Tree be dead.

---

5 Compare the foregoing scene with this extract from a deleted chapter of the novel *Father Adam*, entitled 'Eva Keynes' (Powys's inverted commas):

'Eva Keynes'

It was Mr Punchin who put this name before them, uncovering the inquiry in a detached and far away tone as though he rather feared to adventure his little boat of news into the wide sea of Mr Hinks' imagination.

'No,' said Jeremy, 'thik bain't 'er name now Josiah, she be now called by the name of 'im that be dead.'

'Eva Owlsworth.'

Mr Punchin had hoisted his sail. ''Tis Eva Owlsworth after thik Charley be dead and done wi' in war.'

To show his appreciation of his friend's wisdom Mr Hinks slowly and pointedly nodded after the departing figure of the keeper and then as slowly said as though he were giving out the text of a sermon, 'After thik died she do bide wi' 'e.' . . . They also recalled the days when Charley Owlsworth as a little boy used to run after Eva Keynes, and the times even before that when the keeper used to come to Church with his young wife. (*FA*2, 133–4)

JOHN PUNCHIN

May be the lightning 'ave killed tree.

THOMAS HINKS

There be a nesty up tree.

WALTER HINDS

An some'at else do hang there.

WILLIAM SPOKES

'Tis a cap I do fancy.

JOHN PUNCHIN

'Tis queer to think that any living body did hang 'is cap up thik dead tree.

THOMAS HINKS

Tree be dead.

WILLIAM SPOKES

Dead tree be.

JOHN PUNCHIN

Wood be ~~green~~ pretty now.

WALTER HINDS

True ~~true~~ John we be at hay work now, soon 't will be harvesting, and then weed burning time will come.

THOMAS HINKS

Then there will be root pulling, and there will be ice in the mangel leaves, and after that hedging time will come.

JOHN PUNCHIN

When hedging be done corn sowing do begin.[6]

WILLIAM SPOKES

An' when we bain't hay making or harvesting we be ploughing.

WALTER HINDS

True ~~true~~ William.

---

[6] Powys writes from personal experience; he farmed in Norfolk and Suffolk between 1892 and 1901.

WILLIAM SPOKES

There be no end to work, no sooner we be out of one thing than we be into t'other.

THOMAS HINKS

There be always something to do at home as well as in field for farmer.

JOHN PUNCHIN

True thee be Thomas, only last night I went into me woodshed and roof fell in.

WALTER HINDS

~~True true~~ Our houses do fall upon us, all things do decay.[7]

THOMAS HINKS

Our lives be all one long funeral service.

WALTER HINDS

True ~~true~~ Walter.

JOHN PUNCHIN

Seeing they two under tree do make ~~me~~ I mind things.

~~WALTER HINDS~~

~~True true.~~

~~JOHN PUNCHIN~~

I do mind—only ~~*too too*~~ many harvests do come between—I do mind taking a young maiden into wood when I were young.

WILLIAM SPOKES

'Tis best to forget they times.

WALTER HINDS

True ~~true~~ 'tis best.

THOMAS HINKS

Where be thik maiden now?

JOHN PUNCHIN

Up alongside of wold yew tree in Church Yard.

---

7 'By much slothfulness the building decayeth; and through idleness of the hands the house droppeth through.' (Ecclesiastes x.18), with perhaps a glance at 'All Things Decay and Die' (title of a poem by Robert Herrick [1591–1674]).

WILLIAM SPOKES

Our old women still be living.

JOHN PUNCHIN

Our old women wish we to die first.

THOMAS HINKS

There bain't nor drink up at Inn.

~~WALTER HINDS (*sorrowfully*)~~

~~True true.~~

WILLIAM SPOKES

Landlord 'ave put up notice on's gate that there bain't nor beer in's cellar.

JOHN PUNCHIN

I did see as I were a-loading the great waggon the brewer's van going up road to Inn.

WALTER HINDS

Thee mid 'ave told I thik news before—I be a-going.

[*Exeunt countrymen.*

Enter four old countrywomen from the fields, they are wearing sunbonnets and have ~~evidently~~ been haymaking, they walk wearily as though they were on the lookout for snakes. They each carry a few sticks that they have found. They stop just where the old countrymen had ~~stopped~~ stood and turn to the lovers, ~~who still remain deep plunged in the golden waters of love's exquisite sea.~~ who lie together very still.]

MOTHER PUNCHIN

Look 'ee there, 'tis some fun they two be out for.

MOTHER HINDS

No no they be only holding one another.

MOTHER HINKS(*with contempt*)

Charley Owlsworth 'e be too soft ~~'e be~~ an' too clever, 'e be.

MOTHER SPOKES

He he, but 'e do let a kiss en.

MOTHER PUNCHIN (*disdainfully*)

A kiss bain't nothing.

MOTHER HINDS

A kiss do begin things.

MOTHER HINKS

May be 'tis ended.

MOTHER SPOKES

'Twill be some'at for Enmore if she be caught.

MOTHER PUNCHIN

I do mind coming to wood when I were young.

MOTHER HINDS

He he, 'tis a pity they do stay so still.

MOTHER PUNCHIN

I do like to watch a bit of fun.

MOTHER HINDS

We all do like that. He he, when 'tis winter dark they men don't always know we be so wold as we be.

MOTHER PUNCHIN

~~Girls~~ Maids be careful now not to get catched.

MOTHER HINKS

They do learn about things up at school they do.

MOTHER HINDS

'Tis learning that do spoil fun.

MOTHER SPOKES

They don't stir now, they ~~do only hold hands~~ be soft.

Wood be a poor place for stick gathering, 'tis only these few I've a-got.

MOTHER PUNCHIN

'Twere better if all wood were like thik dead tree.

MOTHER HINKS

Dead wood be best for we.

MOTHER HINDS

Dead wood be best.

MOTHER SPOKES

~~Lovers' meetings~~ Chaps and maids do give us food for talk.

MOTHER PUNCHIN

We Enmore folk don't live by bread alone.[8]

MOTHER HINKS

We do live by talk. Me wold man do 'ear some'at up at pub 'e do.

MOTHER SPOKES

~~Thik Mr Neville do tell~~ Parson do tell we to love one another, 'e do tell we to love our neighbour.[9] See they two.

MOTHER PUNCHIN

Who be our neighbour? [10]

MOTHER SPOKES

No one that we do know.

MOTHER HINDS

'Tis well there be ~~malice~~ badness in world.

MOTHER HINKS

'Tis well there be sin.

MOTHER PUNCHIN

'Tis well there be death.

MOTHER SPOKES

No no death be a mistake.

MOTHER HINDS

What do thee mean Mother Spokes?

MOTHER SPOKES

We don't want to die.

MOTHER PUNCHIN

We are best talking.

---

8 'Man shall not live by bread alone, but by every word that proceedeth out of the mouth of God.' (Matthew iv.4)

9 'thou shalt love thy neighbour as thyself' (Leviticus xix.18 and Matthew xxii.39, etc)

10 From the parable of the good Samaritan: 'But he, willing to justify himself, said unto Jesus, And who is my neighbour?' (Luke, x.29)

MOTHER HINKS

'Tis a fine village for talk.

MOTHER SPOKES

He he, I did meet Mary Keyne t'other day, and I did advise she to enjoy herself. 'Thee'll only live once,' I did say, 'an' kisses don't taste sweet when we be old.'

MOTHER HINDS

What else did you say to she?

MOTHER SPOKES

~~He he,~~ I did tell her that the trouble young girls be so ashamed of don't always come.

MOTHER HINKS

He he, Mother Spokes do know.

MOTHER HINDS

Mother Spokes do know.

MOTHER PUNCHIN

Mother Spokes do know.

MOTHER SPOKES

You should 'ave seen maiden blush when I did tell she.

MOTHER HINDS

Young girls do blush when we married folk do talk.

MOTHER HINKS [11]

Sin be good.

MOTHER PUNCHIN

If we listened to ~~Mr Neville~~ Parson there would be no pleasure in life.

MOTHER SPOKES [12]

'Tis nice to tell they young ~~girls~~ maids what ~~they~~ men folk do do.

MOTHER HINDS

'Tis nice to teach the ~~young~~ children about things.

---

11 Ams has *Hinds* again.
12 Ams has *Punchin* again.

MOTHER HINKS

'Tis nice to see they snigger and laugh.

MOTHER PUNCHIN

Our wold men did go up field path to Inn, most like drink be come.

MOTHER SPOKES

We best follow they.

MOTHER HINDS

A drop of drink be good for we too.

[*Exeunt old country~~men~~ women going the same way that the men have taken. Mary Keyne and Charley Owlsworth rise ~~they~~ and embrace ~~long and lovingly~~.*

Charley Owlsworth ~~gently but firmly~~ unclasps her arms that are about his neck and picks up his bundle. He looks round once as he leaves the stage and stands for a moment watching Mary who is leaning against the dead tree weeping.][13]

~~[*Exit Charley Owlsworth.*~~

~~*After a short pause Mr Neville enters walking slowly.*~~

~~*Mr Neville wears a worn black overcoat, he looks like a man who has seen trouble. He is old and careworn, but about him there is an aura that we*~~[14]

~~me to go back. A voice calls to me out of the dead tree. The voice is Charley's voice he bids me come—Yes I must go.~~

~~MR NEVILLE~~

~~[*holding her firmly*] No you shall not go. I am your guardian now. You shall not go.~~

~~[*Turns fiercely to the dead tree.*]~~

~~In the holy name of Christ cease your evil willing.~~

~~[*The green leaves near to the dead tree move as though a sudden gust of wind has ruffled them, and an evil laugh is faintly heard. Mary allows herself to be led away weeping.*]~~

Curtain

---

13 Powys here writes *end of Scene 1*

14 At this point 5 Ams leaves have been cut out.

SCENE ~~Act~~ II

~~Seven~~ ~~Six months have passed since the first Act. The season is now winter. The heath of Enmore has yielded herself up to the embrace of the cold dark months.~~

~~But though nature hath become cold man is still blessed with the warmth of love.~~

~~The scene is the interior of the cottage of Keeper Owlsworth. This homely room is all neatness warmth and order. It is clear that tender feminine hands love and work there.~~

Scene: The kitchen of the keeper's cottage. The time is evening.

The brass at the end of the stock of an old muzzle loading gun shines as though just cleaned. The ~~old~~ bureau shows off its old oak to the best advantage, and the dresser with the willow pattern plates thereon gives a ~~sense~~ feeling of ~~homely~~ peace and comfort. A kettle that hangs suspended by a chain over the hearth fire is singing.

On one side of the fire there is a settle, upon the other there is a high-backed oaken chair upon which Keeper Owlsworth is sitting. Keeper Owlsworth is dressed in woodland clothes, he wears his working boots upon which moss and lichen have adhered.

Keeper Owlsworth is an old man, slightly bent but wiry. He is like a gnarled root. His adopted daughter Mary Keyne or Mary Owlsworth as she is sometimes called in the village stands at the table and is busy cutting the bread and butter. She wears an apron. The tea is ready set and there are three plates laid out.

One of the plates—a child's—has a border of painted rabbits, with a painted hare sitting up in the middle. Beside this child's plate there is a mug of the same pattern.

There are three wooden chairs placed ready.

Mary Keyne fetches the kettle from the fire and makes the tea.

MARY ~~OWLSWORTH~~ KEYNE

Charley's tea is quite ready Father.

[*Keeper Owlsworth rises slowly from his chair and sits down at the table.*]

KEEPER OWLSWORTH

Charley boy be always late 'e be. Foolish boy when maiden be so good at tea making. [*Looks admiringly at Mary Keyne and rubs his hands in silent glee. After he has eaten two or three mouthfuls Keeper Owlsworth looks anxiously at the window. Mary Keyne rises from her place and goes to the fire, she moves the kettle forward a little and rakes the sticks together upon the hearth, for a moment she leans thoughtfully over the fire.*

Over the ~~aged~~ keeper's face has come a ~~pained~~ doubtful expression as he looks at the window, as though certain unwished-for thoughts ~~had~~ have come into his mind.]

KEEPER OWLSWORTH

Be they trees cut down in wood?

MARY KEYNE

Yes Father, the new Squire has had the trees cut down.

KEEPER OWLSWORTH

Me Charley boy ~~never went~~ bain't gone to no war ~~did~~ be 'e?

MARY KEYNE

Oh no, Charley be all right, Charley will come in soon. ~~I almost fancy now that I can hear his merry voice.~~ [*Keeper Owlsworth laughs a queer crackling laugh like the breaking of little forest twigs.*]

KEEPER OWLSWORTH

Ah ha, she do know where Charley do bide, trust maiden for knowing. Mary do know what me boy be up to, a fine woman she'll be to me boy wi' all her working ways. [*Keeper Owlsworth still looks with pride at Mary.*]

She don't go out nowhere after chaps she don't, she do only sometimes go to Church to hear parson preach.

[*Keeper Owlsworth's look changes as though he remembers a calamity that has happened.*] Wood be cut down bain't ~~it~~ en?

MARY KEYNE

Yes Father, Squire Robinson has had the wood felled.

KEEPER OWLSWORTH

Charley's cap be there still?

MARY KEYNE

Yes Father, Charley's cap is there, the tree with the ~~hawk's~~ raven's nest was too thin and bent to be any good to the woodmen, so they let that tree stay.

[*The old man moves his head from side to side and mutters.*]

KEEPER OWLSWORTH

They poaching devils have beat I at last, wold Keeper Owlsworth be beat at last. All ~~my~~ me life long I've kept they poachers out of ~~me~~ wood, and now they've been so bold as to take wood itself away.

MARY KEYNE

You must eat your tea, Father.

KEEPER OWLSWORTH

[*looking curiously at the girl.*] You be Charley's maiden bain't 'e? Be Charley's tea ready?

MARY KEYNE

Yes Father. [*Mary Keyne points to the vacant chair.*]

KEEPER OWLSWORTH

Charley be gone out long 'e be.

MARY KEYNE

Yes Father.

KEEPER OWLSWORTH

Be Charley out on heath?

MARY KEYNE

Charley said he was going to Norfolk to buy the pheasant eggs.

KEEPER OWLSWORTH

There bain't no pheasant eggs in winter.

MARY KEYNE

It may be for something else that Charley be gone for.

KEEPER OWLSWORTH

Squire sent en?

MARY KEYNE

Yes Father.

KEEPER OWLSWORTH

They noise-making devils 'ave gone too that cut down wood.

MARY KEYNE

Yes Father, they're all gone.

KEEPER OWLSWORTH

An' wood be gone.

MARY KEYNE

Most of it I fear.

KEEPER OWLSWORTH

What war were they stealing devils a-talking of?

MARY KEYNE

Oh, it was only their fun to talk.

KEEPER OWLSWORTH

I did what I could to keep they out of wood. I stood up ~~to they~~ in gateway an' I never moved until they devils dragged I out of road to let thik engine go by.

Devil's 'twere. She Devils amongst they. Satan 'is woon self up in Engine.

[*Very sadly*] Wood be felled,[15] poacher devils have taken wood. Wood be moved, evil creatures 'ave taken wood. Where did bide wold Keeper Owlsworth that he never shot they ugly things? Keeper were coward-like not to shoot at they, only 'e did think that shots could never hurt they evil ones. Keeper Owlsworth could not stop thik engine wi' Satan aboard en.

MARY KEYNE

Don't you trouble too much about the wood Father, you have the heath still to look to.

KEEPER OWLSWORTH

[*looks intently at Mary.*] What war were they poaching Devils a-talking of? … Me Charley bain't gone to no war be 'e?

MARY KEYNE

[*looking towards the window*] Charley's gone to Norfolk Father.

---

[15] Here ends the BC Eb, which, according to Michel Pouillard in his article 'T. F. Powys and the Theatre', is also the end of the play. His resulting unfavourable criticisms and mistakes are based on his having read only the first third of the play—for details see *SEW* cvi–cvii.

KEEPER OWLSWORTH (*slowly*)

Why don't Charley come home along, 'tain't no good 'e buying pheasants for wood now wood be gone.

~~MARY KEYNE~~

~~Mr Neville knows about Charley, Father.~~

~~KEEPER OWLSWORTH (*chuckling*)~~

~~Oh Eh Mr Neville be the one to know, 'tain't much Mr Neville don't know...But all'same Keeper Owlsworth bain't nor indoor servant to rest all evening idle.~~ I must go me rounds now, I must after they poachers. I haven't lived on Enmore Heath all these years without knowing what they be out an' after. I do know well enough that they poachers do watch for I to go in to me meals.

[*The old man rises leaving his tea hardly tasted and goes out of the house.*

Mary Keyne rises too and clears away the tea things.

A knock is heard at the door.

~~*Enter Mr Neville. Mr Neville, who seems sadder, and who stoops more, hands Mary Keyne*~~ *An official envelope is handed to Mary by a child.*]

~~MR NEVILLE~~ THE CHILD

The postman saw me as I was ~~coming here~~ playing this morning and asked me to give you this letter. Mother did open en.

[*Exit child. Mary Keyne ~~opens~~ takes the letter with trembling fingers, reads only a line or two, and sinks weeping upon the settle. The letter falls on the floor.*

~~MR NEVILLE~~

~~You can never be sure Mary, there is a hope, a chance, some have come home even after they have been named in the list of the fallen.~~

~~My child you must not despair, deep below all this terror and human woe there is the deep sea, the sea of eternity that is always still. Plunge your sad thoughts into that sea. In that sea there is sadness too but it is not human our sadness, it is made beautiful because the holy dead know it, because the holy dead dwell in it ...~~

~~Mary we must hide our hearts' sorrows from the old man ... Charley wished it to be so, it is proper that we should respect his wishes.~~

Keeper Owlsworth enters. Mary Keyne calms herself and is busy about the fire placing sticks so that they may burn.]

KEEPER OWLSWORTH

'Tis strange, 'tis strange, I did see they poachers coming out of wood, an' they did turn into Deadman's Lane. I did watch they, thinking that they would go out on to heath.

'Tis strange, 'tis strange they did pass on by side track that be the right road to this very howes. Some'at be wrong wi' world when poachers take the path to~~wards~~ keeper's cottage.

I did come across wood and be got in first, 'tis strange for I do believe they poachers be coming to see I.

~~[*Keeper Owlsworth turns to*~~

[*Enter the four old countrymen John Punchin, William Spokes, Thomas Hinks and Walter Hinds. The countrymen* ~~*look in a dazed way*~~ *blink at the lamp upon the table, as men will* ~~*look*~~ *when they are come out of the darkness into the light.*]

JOHN PUNCHIN

'Tain't often we be come so far as Keeper's cottage.

WILLIAM SPOKES

We most times stay by wold village wall.

WALTER HINDS

Tonight we thought we'd step so far as Keeper's.

THOMAS HINKS

We were minded to see wood that be cut down.

[*The countrymen sit themselves upon the settle before the fire. The keeper is sitting upon the other side of the fire in his oak chair. Mary is busy putting the room in order.* ~~*Mr Neville stands by the table and is looking into the fire. There is silence in the room, each man bows his head as though doubt and trouble are in the air.*~~]

~~THOMAS HINKS~~

~~[*pointing with his finger.*] Thick be Mr Neville.~~

~~[*The countrymen turn their heads and look curiously at Mr Neville.*]~~

JOHN PUNCHIN

[*watching Mary Keyne's movements*] Thik be Mary Keyne.

WILLIAM SPOKES

No, 'tis Mary Owlsworth.

WALTER HINDS

No, 'tis plain Mary.

JOHN PUNCHIN

Keeper be looking well though wood be down.

THOMAS HINKS (*in a louder tone*)

'Tain't much for thee to do now, Keeper.

WILLIAM SPOKES

Summer green be gone now.

JOHN PUNCHIN

Winter time be come.

WALTER HINDS

I do mind springtime I do, I were leaning over heath gate when cuckoo bought 'is voice at Shelton fair.

WILLIAM SPOKES

I were wi' thee then ~~John~~ Walt.

WALTER HINDS

True thee be William, an' a courting couple passed we and the first swallows flew by.

WILLIAM SPOKES

I do mind thik spring day, there were a cooing dove in wood amongst they green trees.

THOMAS HINKS

I do mind they spring days too, I never had to stop horses then to clean me wold plough, plough did go easy in furrow. 'Tis different now damp mists be come.

JOHN PUNCHIN

Yes, they spring days be gone, I were doing a bit of hedging then and I do mind telling farmer that it weren't right to cut off they green sproutings. 'Young things should grow,' I did say to en … but it be different now.

KEEPER OWLSWORTH

[*turning towards the countrymen and looking strangely at them*] What be ~~you~~ thee come for, what be ~~you~~ thee come for? For years and years all the folk of Enmore have been a-feared of Keeper Owlsworth. No one have ever spoke to I, all village be afraid. ~~of I.~~ 'Tis strange that thee be come, may be last day be a-coming now wood be felled.

JOHN PUNCHIN

Nothing have happened to we, Keeper.

WALTER HINDS

'Tisn't we that be dead.

THOMAS HINKS

'Tisn't we that be dead.

MARY KEYNE

~~[*with a catch in her voice*]~~ Don't don't, please don't tell. You know you only came to see the wood that's been cut down.

JOHN PUNCHIN

'Tisn't all cut down.

WALTER HINDS

~~Hawk's~~ Raven's nestie be still there.

THOMAS HINKS

Near to ~~hawk's~~ nestie there be a boy's cap hung up.

JOHN PUNCHIN

[*to Keeper Owlsworth*] Where be thee's boy Charley now?

KEEPER OWLSWORTH

Charley be out on heath or else 'e be gone to Norfolk.

WALTER HINDS

'Tisn't we that be dead.

~~M[R] NEVILLE~~

~~I am going to the village neighbours, that is your way too, for company sake we may as well go together, you see the night [*points to the window*] is very dark.~~

~~[*The countrymen consider this project for a moment in silence.*]~~

JOHN PUNCHIN

Dark night be come, 'tis time we did go.

WALTER HINDS

'Tain't we that be dead, we only called to see how 'twere wi' 'ee neighbour.

WILLIAM SPOKES

We did but come so far to see wood that be felled.

THOMAS HINKS

We did just step up to say that none of we weren't dead.

[*The countrymen slowly rise from the settle, concentrate their gaze for a moment upon the lamp as though to store up light for their journey and exeunt.* ~~*in company with Mr Neville who leads the way.*~~]

MARY KEYNE

[*after a moment's complete silence*] Father, I can hear voices outside.

[*Mary Keyne stands by the window, Keeper Owlsworth remains in his high-backed chair. The voices sound as though they are in the lane outside. They are easily distinguished as being the voices of the old countrywomen, although the old women are not seen.*]

MOTHER PUNCHIN

Me wold man were going out to chop wood in shed. I did 'ear 'e chop chop, once twice and then all were silent. Then I did know.

MOTHER HINDS

What did 'e know?

MOTHER PUNCHIN

That me wold man were gone up to '~~Sailor's~~ Soldier's[16] Return'.

MOTHER SPOKES

Wold Spokes went out to chain up 'is dog.

MOTHER HINKS

Thomas went out to feed 'is pig.

MOTHER HINDS

Walter went out after a cow that 'e did tell I was a-mooen' in lane.

---

16 The 'Sailor's Return' inn, somewhat enlarged, is still in Powys's village of Chaldon.

MOTHER HINKS

There weren't no cow an' me pig were fed.

MOTHER SPOKES

Dog were in's kennel.

MOTHER PUNCHIN

Sticks were chopped.

MOTHER SPOKES

An' we followed they up to Inn and we followed they up to Keeper's.

MOTHER HINKS

And as we came up along heath road they went down along Deadman's Lane.

[*Mary Keyne moves across the room and stands near Keeper Owlsworth's chair.*

Mother Punchin's face appears at the window.]

MOTHER PUNCHIN

Keeper do have a good fire in's house.

MOTHER HINKS

Who be there, who be there?

MOTHER PUNCHIN

'Tisn't all the room that I do see.

MOTHER HINDS

Be Mary Keyne in room?

MOTHER PUNCHIN

Postman's letter be on floor.

MOTHER HINKS

Do maid Mary look pale?

MOTHER PUNCHIN

Yes yes she do look pale.

MOTHER SPOKES

What clothes be she in?

MOTHER PUNCHIN

She do wear a long apron.

MOTHER HINDS

He he, I do know what thik be for.

MOTHER SPOKES

She don't want to show her shape, she don't.

MOTHER HINKS

Wold Mother Spokes do know, he he.

MOTHER PUNCHIN

Do thee mind summer evening in wood?

MOTHER HINDS

They did lie close to thik dead tree.

MOTHER SPOKES

She did kiss en, chaps don't stop at nothing when maids do kiss. [*Mary Keyne leans over Keeper Owlsworth's chair and holds her hands over her ears.*]

MOTHER PUNCHIN

That pretty summer fun must be paid for in darksome days.

MOTHER HINDS

Little folk begin to grow in springtime.

MOTHER HINKS

And in winter sorrow be born.

MOTHER SPOKES

'Tis fun for we.
~~[*In sudden fear*] Be Mr Neville in Keeper's room?~~

~~MOTHER PUNCHIN~~

~~He mid be sitting on settle mid may be.~~

~~MOTHER SPOKES~~

~~'Tis Mr Neville that do stop our fun.~~

~~MOTHER HINDS~~

~~Mr Neville bain't nor good to we poor folk.~~

~~MOTHER HINKS~~

~~He do only read they books.~~

MOTHER PUNCHIN

Do 'ee mind dead tree in wood?

MOTHER HINDS

Yes yes, and now others be dead. Shall we go in an' tell wold man who be dead?

~~MOTHER SPOKES~~

~~Mr Neville do say in Village that no one must tell 'e, 'twill break his heart if he do know it.~~

Peep in again Mother Punchin and see what thik maid be doing?

MOTHER PUNCHIN

She do stand ~~sorrowful like~~ sad against chair, as though she's a hidden trouble to think ~~of~~ on.

MOTHER HINKS

'Tis fun for we when young ~~girls~~ maids be caught, wi' all their sweet kissing ways they do cry at the last.

MOTHER SPOKES

'Tis well chaps be bold a-courting, 'tis well they don't stop their fun for a maiden's ~~tears~~ cries.[17]

~~MOTHER HINDS~~

~~'Tis a nice world.~~

~~[*The sound of a voice comes out of the deep darkness that is behind the old women.*]~~

~~THE VOICE~~

~~'Tis a nice world.~~

~~MOTHER PUNCHIN (*fearfully*)~~

~~Who did speak then?~~

---

17 The four prurient countrywomen are fore-runners of Mrs Vosper in their hatred of young girls, and in their provoking and gloating over the seduction and ruin of young maidens. Compare this with the opening of Chapter 13 of *Mr. Weston's Good Wine*:

> Mrs Vosper lived very high in the excitement of life. She lived upon the mountain called Lust. And there she fed happily upon the act of the beast, that is likewise—as we are taught by the wise, as well as by Mr Bunce—the act of God.
>
> But Mrs Vosper hated her own sex, and she wished to do two things with them—to bring them into trouble, and to amuse herself by watching their undoing.

~~MOTHER HINDS~~

~~'Twasn't I.~~

~~MOTHER HINKS~~

~~Nor I.~~

~~MOTHER SPOKES~~

~~Nor I.~~

~~THE VOICE~~

~~'Tis a nice world.~~

MOTHER PUNCHIN

'Tis best we should go, ~~thik voice do speak out of dead tree.~~ afore Keeper do come.

[*Exeunt old countrywomen.*

After the countrywomen are gone the lamp in the keeper's kitchen burns dim for a moment and then goes out. The fire gives but a fitful light to the room.

In the outer darkness seen through the uncurtained window ~~a light shines for a moment. The light shows~~ is[18] *the dim outline of the dead tree.*]

~~THE VOICE~~

~~She is mine, mine mine.~~

~~[*Mr Neville, who is unseen and whose voice also comes from the*~~[19] ~~*he regards her merely as a little child who has broken a toy.*]~~

~~MR NEVILLE~~

~~[*looking down upon the old man and the weeping girl.*]~~

~~There is one living truth in the world—sorrow. All else fades and passes, all else satiates, all else turns into weariness of the flesh. It is sorrow alone that feeds and fills the heart of man.~~

Curtain

[18] *is* is an editorial addition.

[19] At this point one leaf has been torn out.

~~ACT III~~ SCENE III

Scene: The wood. *~~A week has passed~~*

It is the afternoon of a winter's day. Destruction and devastation have fallen upon the once beautiful wood. Broken fir boughs like dead men's bones lie scattered here and there. For the most part these boughs lie trodden into the mud, but a few stick up out of the earth just as they broke off when the trees fell.

There are also a few shrunken and starved bushes unworthy to be called trees that have not been cut down. In sunken places there are pools of dark water. In the midst of this dismal scene the dead tree with the ~~hawk's~~ raven's nest is still standing.

Against the trunk of this tree Mary Keyne is seen to be kneeling as though in prayer.

Enter the four old countrywomen who begin to pick up bits of stick that they put into their aprons. They are so busy looking for the best sticks that they do not at first see Mary Keyne.

MOTHER SPOKES

'Tis well for we that trees be down.

MOTHER PUNCHIN

War time bain't too bad for we, there be dead sticks to gather.

MOTHER HINDS

They do say in Village that Charley Owlsworth were buried in's clothes in they foreign parts.

MOTHER HINKS

I do mind Charley being christened in Enmore Church.

MOTHER PUNCHIN

So do I, so do I, and thik gown 'e did wear me sister made ~~it~~ en.

MOTHER SPOKES

Keeper Owlsworth do think Charley be gone to Norfolk.

MOTHER HINDS

I do mind Keeper when 'e were a boy.

MOTHER HINKS

I do mind Keeper's wife that be dead.

MOTHER PUNCHIN

Me maid Grace do lie under dirt next to she.

MOTHER SPOKES

Church Yard be full.

MOTHER HINDS

True so 'tis and they do say that Parson have a map of Church Yard wi' folk's coffins marked in en.

MOTHER PUNCHIN

True he has that, for Sexton showed it I an' there be only room under corner nettles.

MOTHER HINDS

When wold witch Fan were buried I did look at heap of dirt Sexton had cast up, and I did see a skull in en.

MOTHER HINKS

'Twere wold Barker's most like.[20]

MOTHER SPOKES

I've seen thik skull a-laughing when wold Barker lived.

MOTHER PUNCHIN

He could drink a glass.

MOTHER HINDS

He could sing a song.

MOTHER HINKS

He could kiss a maid.[21]

MOTHER PUNCHIN

There bain't room for we in Church Yard.

MOTHER SPOKES

We don't want to hurry ourselves to go there, 'twould be rudeness to ask they dead folk to move for we.

---

[20] 'The Candle and the Slow-Worm' (*Fables*) includes mention of 'a rat who was making a nest in Mr Barker's grave', and in *The Market Bell* (p.43) there is 'Sexton Truggin, who had broken his pick against a great stone that he had mistaken for his friend Barker's skull and so struck hard to please himself'.

[21] See Hamlet on Yorick: *Hamlet*, Act V, Shakespeare.

MOTHER PUNCHIN

You know 'tis said that if any one go up into Church porch on the last night of the old year, they do see the folk that are to die come in.[22]

MOTHER HINKS

So 'tis said.

MOTHER HINDS

I've heard the same told.

MOTHER PUNCHIN

I did do it neighbours.

MOTHER SPOKES

You never did sure.

MOTHER PUNCHIN

Yes I were minded to see with me own eyes the folk moping in to die.

MOTHER SPOKES (*anxiously*)

Thee never see'd I did 'e?

MOTHER HINDS

Nor I?

MOTHER HINKS

Nor I?

MOTHER PUNCHIN

We'd been having a bit of a rumpus thik night me wold man and I. And he being the stronger did put I out of door and did lock up house.

Poor wold man 'e had a drop of drink in's head.

Out in road all were white and they stars were a-shining. The thatch on farmer's barn were white wi' snow. Oh 'twas cold in road, and stars were fixed and frozen up in sky. I weren't best pleased neither to be in lane with me wold man snug in bed under blankets.

'Twere then that I thought as I'd like to see who were to die, and I walked to Church and in through gate and up path between tombs, and stood in porch.

22 This superstition is the theme of Powys's tale 'The Midnight Hour', which was published in *Everyman*, 23 February, 1934, *London-World News Weekly* New Series No. 22, and in *Three Short Stories*, The Dud Noman Press, Loughton, 1971.

Thik head above porch, though it were but of stone[23] did gleam at I as I did pass under en. And so I did wait till the hour drew near, thinking to me self that I'd soon see one of you a-coming.

Then the clock struck and a white owl flew out of Church tower,[24] and I did see something coming up path. 'Twere old Keeper Owlsworth that did come. He did come up path a-laughing at some'at, you do know the way he do laugh same as dry twigs cracking.

MOTHER HINDS

We do know.

MOTHER PUNCHIN

He did come near to I and then passed out amongst graves, and I heard his laugh under yew tree for the last time.

I were just going to leave Church porch when I did see two more folks a-coming. These two were man and maid and were a-holding to one another.

MOTHER HINKS

Did 'ee know who 'twere?

MOTHER PUNCHIN

I did know he anyways, 'twas Charley Owlsworth, but the maid's looks I did never see, because her face were all bloodied.

---

23 Powys's early allegory *The Second Child* has:

> Carved upon the lych-gate there is the head of an ugly demon or human monstrosity. It is carved in hard stone and as the legends go, has been in the village since the time of the Romans.
>
> The most ancient of all the village stories speaks with horror of a terrible thing, half man and half beast, that lived in the old Roman mansion, and was the son of a depraved Roman noble, about this matter the demon himself is quite silent, and the only sign of life he gives is to smile when a funeral passes below, or to frown when the merry sound of the wedding bell awakens sighs from the old church tower.

Ams, HRC. Extracts from *The Second Child,* of which this quotation is not a part, are in *SEW* xxxiv; extracts, 5–20.

24 Cf. Owen Wingrave's death in *Cottage Shadows* (*SEW* lxxv–lxxvii; complete 369–433): 'It was nearly dark and I opened the window as we Lenton folks do when there's a death. Outside on the green our little Fanny was waiting with some boys—bad boys most like. They were standing watching young Wingrave's window—"To see the white bird fly out,"— they told I.'

MOTHER SPOKES

How did Charley look, were his face same like?

MOTHER PUNCHIN

To tell truth I didn't fancy staring at 'e much, but all'same I thought I see'd a red hole in's forehead.

MOTHER HINDS

I be glad thee never saw I.

MOTHER SPOKES

Don't thee go to Church porch again Mother Punchin.

MOTHER HINKS

Thee mid see thee's woon self next time.

MOTHER PUNCHIN

'Tis best to live.

MOTHER SPOKES

The dead bain't good for company.

MOTHER HINDS

No, they bain't nice people to meet at night time.

MOTHER SPOKES

I can't pick up one more stick, me apron be full.
[*Mother Spokes looks up and sees Mary Keyne who is kneeling with her hands over her eyes. Mary Keyne rises to her feet and looks this way and that as though to find a way of escape. The old women stand round her and look at her maliciously. Mary Keyne throws her arms round the dead tree.*]

MOTHER PUNCHIN

'Tis a pretty maiden.

MOTHER HINDS

I wonder whether what they do say in village be true?

MOTHER HINKS

They do say that there be some'at the matter with thik pretty maid.

MOTHER SPOKES

I've heard same story told.

MOTHER PUNCHIN

He he.
[*Mary Keyne holds the dead tree as though she is crying to it to save her from the old women.*]

MOTHER HINDS

Dead tree won't hide your shape me pretty.

MOTHER HINKS

Maiden do look pale, he he.

MOTHER PUNCHIN

She've finished her summer fun maiden have.

MOTHER SPOKES

'Tis our fun now.

MOTHER HINDS

Let's catch hold of she and find out what be the matter.

MOTHER PUNCHIN

We'll soon know.

MOTHER SPOKES

You take she hold Mother Punchin.
[*The old women laugh, and ~~an evil laugh like theirs seems to come out of the dead tree. The old women~~ approach as though to catch hold of Mary Keyne, who being seized with a sudden ~~terror~~ fear of the tree has started back almost into the arms of the old countrywomen.*

Enter Keeper Owlsworth. As soon as they see the keeper the old countrywomen turn away from Mary Keyne who slips between them and ~~goes off the stage~~ exits without being noticed by Keeper Owlsworth.]

KEEPER OWLSWORTH

[*to the old women*] I've caught you now you stealing thieves.

MOTHER SPOKES

[*in a crooning propitiating voice*] No no, don't 'ee say that Keeper Owlsworth, we bain't what thee do say, we be only getting a stick or two for fire. Thee do know there bain't no railings now wood be down so we folk can walk into wood when we be minded.

MOTHER HINDS

Do 'ee now let thik wold gun rest quiet under thee's arm, Keeper Owlsworth.

We bain't no poachers for thee to shoot at Keeper, we be poor folk, we be out picking up one or two little sticks.

KEEPER OWLSWORTH

Evil times be come to I, evil times be come.

Days do darken now wood be down. They Devils did come with screeching engine and did take wood, and now there be old women come to steal.

MOTHER HINKS

True 'tis we be wold women but we bain't stealing thieves, we be but come for a dry stick or two, Keeper.

[*The far distant boom of a great cannon is heard.*]

KEEPER OWLSWORTH

Queer, queer, 'tis winter time and it do thunder. Or else maybe they ships be shooting at target out at sea.

When last it did thunder there were pheasants to answer in wood. I did see a pheasant too a while ago that should have called, but no pheasant do call.

[*fiercely*] You've drove pheasant away you old women.

MOTHER SPOKES

'Tis a true word that Keeper do say, for we be old women, but all'same we never drove pheasant away.

[*The distant boom of a cannon is heard again.*]

KEEPER OWLSWORTH

'Tis they great ships.

MOTHER HINDS

[*looking up craftily*] No no Keeper, sound don't come from ships.

KEEPER OWLSWORTH (*thoughtfully*)

'Tis thunder then. I do mind when I were a little child hearing thunder in winter, and my father did say—and he was a keeper too—that thunder in winter did mean a death in our family, and sure enough

Mother died before the month were out.

MOTHER PUNCHIN

[*The sound is heard again.*] 'Tisn't thunder we do hear, Keeper Owlsworth.

MOTHER SPOKES

[*looking up at the ~~hawk's~~ raven's nest*] There be a boy's cap hung up there besides nest.

MOTHER HINKS

Sure it be a cap that do hang there.

KEEPER OWLSWORTH

[*places his gun against the tree.*] Yes you old women, 'tis me Charley's cap. Oh ho naughty boy that he were to climb up tree. Didn't I tell Charley never to climb thik tree, and there's his cap to show I that 'e've a-climbed en. Ah young boys be gamesome creatures. I do mind me woon father telling I never to climb up Hardy's tower on hill because the steps be worn in en, but blessed if I didn't climb en the next Sunday. [*The old countrywomen laugh.*]

MOTHER SPOKES

Keeper be pleased 'e be.

KEEPER OWLSWORTH (*more kindly*)

Thee do know good folk, that me son be gone to Norfolk to buy pheasants for good Squire Crew. [*Looks sadly round him.*] Oh to think that Devils should have come and cut wood down, poor wold Squire Crew will sorrow and sigh[25] when he do see en.

MOTHER PUNCHIN

Squire Crew be dead.

KEEPER OWLSWORTH

[*draws his hand slowly across his forehead as though he is dazed.*]
Who did say that Squire be dead?

[25] *sorrow and sigh* is reminiscent of 'All the birds of the air fell a-sighing and a-sobbing/ when they heard of the death of poor Cock Robin.' (part of the chorus from an old English nursery rhyme)

MOTHER HINKS

I do mind when Squire Crew were born.

MOTHER HINDS

I do mind when Squire Crew were married.

MOTHER SPOKES

And I do mind when Squire Crew were put under sod.
[*The sound comes again.*]

KEEPER OWLSWORTH

[*as though uncertain*] There be thunder again.

MOTHER HINDS

No Keeper Owlsworth, thik sound be guns.

KEEPER OWLSWORTH

They ships at sea.

MOTHER HINKS

No no 'tis guns where war be.

MOTHER PUNCHIN

Hist hist Mother Hinks, you've been and told Keeper, when maiden did tell we not to say nothing.

KEEPER OWLSWORTH

[*in the voice of one upon whom the ~~evil~~ thing he has most feared has fallen*] Me boy Charley bain't gone to no war be 'e?

MOTHER SPOKES

'Tis best for 'ee to know it, Charley be killed.
[*Keeper Owlsworth covers his face with his hands and leans against the dead tree. ~~he expresses the sorrow of a father who knows that he has lost his only son.~~*]

MOTHER HINDS

[*smiling and pointing with her finger at the keeper*] Keeper Owlsworth won't mind we now.

MOTHER PUNCHIN

[*shaking her fist*] We be stealing thieves be we.[26]

---

[26] Powys has here deleted a question mark, leaving a full stop.

MOTHER HINKS

Keeper be thoughtful 'e be.

MOTHER SPOKES

Ah we be old women we be.

[*Mother Spokes sees a rabbit dead in a snare, she takes up the rabbit and puts it into her apron amongst the sticks, she goes off the stage chuckling to herself.*]

MOTHER HINKS

He he, Keeper don't see we old women now. I do know where cock pheasant be caught in netting, I do mean to have 'e I do.

MOTHER PUNCHIN

Wood be ours now. I do mind seeing a partridge fallen into bushes, winged may be, I may as well have he to me supper.

MOTHER HINDS

I did see a rabbit with weasel on's track, weasel will kill rabbit for I. [27]

[*Exeunt countrywomen chuckling.*

~~*Enter Mr Neville who walks very slowly with his head bent. Mr Neville does not notice the keeper who has sunk down upon his knees beside the dead tree.*~~

~~*The winter's afternoon is growing dim. Mr Neville sits down upon a broken bough and reads aloud.*~~]

[27] Powys here writes *end of S*

~~ACT IV~~ SCENE IV

Scene: Keeper Owlsworth's cottage the same evening.

The tea table is ready set. There are three places prepared as in ~~Act II~~ Scene II. Mary Keyne is sitting upon the settle hemming a shroud.

Enter Keeper Owlsworth, ~~Keeper Owlsworth is much altered,~~ he looks like death. But it is the figure of a woodland death that he resembles; death in the shape of a gnarled rotted root. Mary Keyne sews on, she does not appear to notice the keeper's entrance. Her looks have also changed. ~~, there is an air of spiritual excitement about her, as though she feels that the true happiness of her life is very near.~~

As she sews she softly sings an old ballad that she learnt at school called 'Barbara Allen's Cruelty'.[28]

KEEPER OWLSWORTH

[*standing beside Mary*] Thee be gladsome tonight maiden.

MARY KEYNE

I'm happy sewing, Father.

KEEPER OWLSWORTH

Sure 'tis a pretty dress thee be making. A dress to wear when summer sun be warm, and when they little small rabbits do play in field.

MARY KEYNE

Oh yes Father, it's a pretty dress.
[*Mary Keyne carefully folds the shroud and places it with her needle and cotton upon the dresser. After doing so she guides the old man to his chair by the tea table.*

Keeper Owlsworth takes up the child's plate and points to the rabbit. He speaks ~~in a strange tone~~ as though he knows that Charley is dead.]

KEEPER OWLSWORTH

'Tis a pretty plate. Why, there be a little rabbit on this little plate.

Me boy Charley bain't gone to no war be 'e?
[*Mary Keyne leans over the table and weeps.*]

---

[28] which begins 'In Scarlet town where I was born / There was a fair maid dwellin''. Mentioned in Pepys's Diary.

MARY KEYNE

Charley, Charley, let me die too, let me die too. I be making me dress Charley.

KEEPER OWLSWORTH

Me boy Charley bain't dead be 'e?

[*Keeper Owlsworth rises with difficulty, he moves to the dresser and takes up the shroud, this he holds up. The garment unfolds itself.*]

'Tis a pretty dress.

[*Mary Owlsworth takes the thing gently ~~but firmly~~ from him and folding it again she replaces it as before. Mary leads the old man back to his chair.*]

MARY KEYNE

Father you must not go the rounds tonight. Most like some old village neighbours will step up to have a chat with you. ~~and there's Mr Neville who may come in~~. Father it's tea time now, you've eaten nothing you know.

[*Keeper Owlsworth refuses to sit by the table, he moves to the window which he tries to open. Mary Keyne opens the window for him, and seeing that he wishes to remain looking out, she moves his high-backed chair near to the window.*

Through the window there is clearly seen the outline of the far hills.

This outline is broken in one place by a solitary tree that rears itself seemingly above the hills.

Upon the top bough of the tree there is a dim object that might be a boy's cap.]

KEEPER OWLSWORTH

[*in broken tones*] I do mind thik wood, I do mind thik wood, afore ever they evil creatures came with their laughter and noise. I can mind wold wood seventy years a-gone.

Vor seventy years they pretty trees 'ave spoke to I, 'ave sung to I.

I were their keeper, and their friend too I were, and every pathway I did know and every little squirrel.

They little small squirrels 'ave come to I, and have climbed on me back and 'ave taken nuts out of my hand.

Yes I do mind those times long a-gone.

I did once carry home one of they merry creatures to show to

Charley when 'e were little.

Once there came a singing nightingale to wood.

And Squire Crew did say, while we bided and listened to its song, that e'd sooner see thik bird in tree than a hundred pheasants.

[*Keeper Owlsworth breaks into an angry tone.*]

Why didn't I stop they ugly things cutting down wood. They were like me woon dear little children they trees were. Many's the day that I've took and swung little Charley in branches while they pheasants went in and out of undergrowth same as hens mid do.

[*For a while Keeper Owlsworth is silent. Mary kneels beside him.*

As though shaken with a sudden terror, he stretches out his hand to the window.]

Dead tree be holding me boy's cap. Oh I would that me boy's cap were in my hands. [*He appears to be listening.*]

There be something that do hold Charley away from me. Thik something be like dead tree, 'tis great and dark with wings like a black raven. I would that I held my boy's cap once more. I do mind seeing Charley's coat once hung up on chair. Charley were ill with the fever and Mother and I did think 'e were gone. I did walk quiet like up to chair and did take up me boy's coat an' I did kiss en.

Oh that I might kiss me boy's cap before I die.

[*Mary Keyne kisses the old man and goes softly out into the night. Keeper Owlsworth lies back in his chair as though exhausted.*

Enter very slowly the stooping work wearied forms of the four old countrymen. They sit upon the settle and lean forward as though they would eat the dying fire.]

JOHN PUNCHIN

'Tis cold.

WALTER HINDS

There be a corpse in fire.

WILLIAM SPOKES

Window be open.

THOMAS HINKS

Now wood be cut down all shelter be gone.

JOHN PUNCHIN

Keeper's chair be moved, why be Keeper's chair moved?

[*Keeper Owlsworth raises his head as though waking out of a deep sleep. He looks through the window with a strained attention, as though he hears some movement outside.*

The old countrymen look round oddly at the keeper.

After a few moments of expectant waiting, the slow thud thud thud of an axe is heard coming from the wood.

Keeper Owlsworth looks round excitedly at the crouching figures of the old men who croon over the fire.]

KEEPER OWLSWORTH

Who be it, who be it? I do hear something in wood. Who be cutting down dead tree in wood?

JOHN PUNCHIN

'Tis cold, 'tis cold, fire be gone out.

WALTER HINDS

Window be open.

WILLIAM SPOKES

Keeper do see something.

THOMAS HINKS

What be it that Keeper do see?

KEEPER OWLSWORTH

~~[*speaking in a strangely excited voice*]~~

May be 'tis Charley, may be 'tis Charley.

Me boy Charley be come home. He he, me boy never went to no war, he he.

Thik little boy be chopping down tree to get 'is cap again.

Don't anyone tell I that me boy be afraid. I said I'd thrash 'e if 'e climbed en. 'Tis a good boy not to go agen is own father.

Now hark to 'e—'tis thik cunning boy that be a-chopping down tree to get 'is own cap back to en.

[*Keeper Owlsworth laughs his old laugh that is like the cracking of dry twigs.*]

Mary Keyne, Mary Keyne.

WILLIAM SPOKES

Keeper be calling maiden because it be cold.

THOMAS HINKS

Window be open, Keeper be calling to someone outside the window.

JOHN PUNCHIN

'Tis strange, 'tis strange, wood be cut down but Keeper be calling to someone in wood.

WILLIAM SPOKES

There be a dead corpse in fire.
[*Enter the four countrywomen very slowly and silently. They stand beside the table. They take no notice of the old men.*]

MOTHER SPOKES

Thik be a pretty plate.

MOTHER HINKS

A nice cup 'tis too.

MOTHER HINDS

Do thee see they little rabbits?

MOTHER PUNCHIN

Thik loaf of bread do look made of fine wheaten flour.

KEEPER OWLSWORTH

Mary Keyne, Mary Keyne.

MOTHER SPOKES

Keeper do call.

MOTHER HINDS

'E do want maiden.

MOTHER HINKS

Who do Keeper want?

MOTHER PUNCHIN

Keeper do call Mary Keyne.
[*The old women stand in silent manner. A manner that gives the impression that they have stood there forever. They almost might have become part*

of the dead things in the room. The old men sit too in silent fashion.

The thud thud of the axe is still heard.

A change has come over Keeper Owlsworth, his face has grown thinner and his voice is more childlike and wistful.]

KEEPER OWLSWORTH

'Tis thee's own husband that be coming Mary. Thee'd best hunt out wedding dress that thee've put away so careful. He he, trust they pretty maidens for knowing where wedding dress do bide.

Me boy Charley will have a good wife neighbours, a good homely wife she'll be. Mary Keyne bain't none of they flighty ones, Mary bain't ashamed of being a servant she bain't.[29] Maid do set no price upon what she do do, she be above money ~~and above price~~ she be.

MOTHER SPOKES

Someone be cutting dead tree in wood.

MOTHER HINDS

Dead branches for we
dead branches for we.[30]

MOTHER HINKS

Someone be working.

MOTHER SPOKES

Who be it that do cut tree in wood?

KEEPER OWLSWORTH

'Tis me boy Charley that be come home. Charley be cutting down dead tree in wood.

[*Keeper Owlsworth raises his head to watch, the topmost boughs of the dead tree are seen to tremble.*

The sound of the axe falling quickens, the branches swing wildly, totter and are gone, leaving only the dark outline of the hills ~~against~~ below the stars.

---

[29] '... the most noble old woman I have ever seen was a servant. ... Mrs Cern's mind was noble and the lowliest things that she did became noble deeds as she did them, she could serve having no desire to be served.' (From Powys's autobiographical piece 'Mrs Cern' [1913], concerning the family servant Mrs Curme [*SEW*, lxix; complete, 311-321])

[30] Powys uses a new line for the chanting repetition.

Mingled with the crash of the falling tree there is a woman's scream. ~~*In the scream there is terror and exaltation.*~~

The fall of the tree is followed by silence, as of death.

~~KEEPER OWLSWORTH *(in a voice like a child's)*~~

~~I do see two figures walking upon hill.~~

~~I do know who they be—'Tis Mary Keyne and me boy Charley. Their clothes do shine same as stars do shine. Maiden's dress be very white, as white as snow that do drift deep in winter time—Me boy Charley do walk with she.~~

~~[*The old man begins to speak as though the two he sees have come nearer to him.*] I be glad thee's come home Charley. [*He stretches out his arms towards the window.*] Me boy Charley be glad to see maiden, there never were any war Charley, there never were any war.~~

~~Yes yes Charley, I'll go back with thee to Norfolk.~~

~~Wood be gone now Charley, I be almost glad that wood be gone, and now I'll come to thee Charley now wood be gone.~~

Keeper Owlsworth sighs ~~happily~~, his head falls back, he is dead.]

MOTHER SPOKES

Keeper be gone to sleep.[31]

[*Mother Spokes takes up the child's cup and hides it in her apron.*]

MOTHER HINKS

Keeper don't see we now.

[*Mother Hinks takes up Charley's plate and hides it in her apron.*]

MOTHER HINDS

Keeper's eyes be open but 'e don't see no one.

[*Mother Hinds takes up the loaf of bread and hides it.*]

MOTHER SPOKES

Keeper do look at stars. Ho ho, Keeper be star gazing.

[*Mother Spokes reaches out for the spoons and hides them.*]

JOHN PUNCHIN

'Tis cold.

---

[31] Within brackets, in thick ink, Llewelyn Powys has added *An' I did peep out of window and Mary be killed by tree falling.* See Afterword: pp. 133 and 140.

WALTER HINDS

Window be open.

THOMAS HINKS

Fire be quite gone out.

WILLIAM SPOKES

I do hear the death beetle ticking.

~~[*Enter Mr Neville who carries in his arms the body of Mary Keyne. Mr Neville lays his burden down beside the keeper's chair.*~~

~~*Mary's hands are clasping a boy's cap.*~~

[*The old women become restless as though they would*[32] *lay their hands upon other things in the room. They move about touching things like birds of prey, and their nails are seen to be long and sharp like poisoned black talons. Exeunt old women.*

The four old countrymen rise from the settle and look at the dead.]

JOHN PUNCHIN

Keeper Owlsworth be dead. ~~'e be.~~
Charley be dead.

WALTER HINDS

Mary Keyne be dead.

THOMAS HINKS

We be ~~alive~~ living.

WILLIAM SPOKES

We be ~~alive~~ living.

THE END

[32] Powys's crossing out continues up to this point, i.e. to the end of the Ams page, evidently overshooting.

AFTERWORD

ABBREVIATIONS

Publications

FA2: Father Adam (novella) 2nd edition
PJ = *The Powys Journal*
PR = *The Powys Review*
SEW: Selected Early Works of T. F. Powys

Descriptions of texts

Ams = authorial manuscript
AmsS = authorial manuscript signed by the author
Eb = Exercise book, soft covers
p = page
pp = pages
RD = rough draft in ink
Tms = typescript not made by the author
Tccms = carbon copy of typescript

Collections

BC = Bissell Collection (now held by The Powys Society and housed in The Dorset County Museum, Dorchester)
HRC = Harry Ransom Humanities Research Center, The University of Texas at Austin

Powys's play 'The Wood' is an interesting and powerful work; I am delighted that it is at last to see the light of day. Ian Robinson is 'amazed at what Powys does with the double chorus of old men and old women and without as far as we know knowing much about the Greek drama. Well, I really think it's genius.'

Of the eight plays which he wrote, Powys grouped three of them together under the title *Three Country Plays*. 'The Wood/ a play in one Act' was written first; judging by internal evidence probably by 1918 (see below), with a later interpolation in Llewelyn Powys's hand added between 1919 and 1920 (see below). Correspondence shows that the second play of the group, a rustic comedy entitled 'Father Adam', was completed by mid-October 1920,[1] and the third play, 'Blind Bartimaeus', according to letters which T. F. wrote to J. C. Powys, in November 1920.[2] 'Father Adam' was published in 2003 in *SEW*, 535–70, and 'Blind Bartimaeus' in 2006 in *PJ* XVI, 121–78.

'Father Adam' seems to have been written more or less easily, the difficult-to-read handwriting of the first draft, with brief interpolations in the margins, running in a continuous block. In the midst of this flow changes of character are sometimes indicated by initials, sometimes not at all. There is little difference of content between the draft and the neat large-hand final version ready to offer for publication.[3] Apart from one sentence in which someone complains that Father Adam says people ought to love one another, 'Father Adam' the play has nothing to do with *Father Adam* the novella, and is the only one of the *Three Country Plays* the material of which Powys does not use elsewhere.

The third play, 'Blind Bartimaeus', survives, as far as I know, only in its large-clear-hand final version. Its main subject is developed in the novel *Mark Only*, which was written two years later.[4] 'Blind Bartimaeus' also contains two themes found in other works—the unpublished early novel *Amos Lear,* written four years earlier (*SEW*, lxxxv–xc; substantial extracts, 471–490), and the later short story 'The Devil' (*The House with the Echo*). For a full and detailed account of Powys's eight plays—including two unfinished ones—see *SEW,* ci–cxvi, and/or my Afterword to 'Blind Bartimaeus' in *PJ* XVI 2006, 173–7.

The evolution of 'The Wood' is complex and closely intertwined with that of the novella *Father Adam.* There is a detailed account of the latter process in my essay 'The Genesis of *Father Adam*' in *FA2*, 105–140. Put briefly, the play's main theme is the history of the Owlsworth family, which is expanded and incorporated into the two versions of the unpublished novel *Father Adam*, finally to become a background feature to the main Father Adam theme of the published novella *Father Adam*. As the war which is in progress in Chapter iii of the novella has ended by Chapter ix, and Powys submitted it to Melrose at the end of 1919, the likely date of composition is 1918–19. In 'The Wood', however, the war does not reach its end, making it probably pre-1918.

In 'Why I Have Given up Writing' (*John O'London's Weekly*, 23 October, 1936) Powys states his writing method as, 'A rough copy first, then a revised version, and a third fair copy to be sent away to the typist.' The process, however, was not always so simple. There is a large amount of material extant from which emerged the final version of the novella *Father Adam*, namely:

Two seed-pieces: 'The Delectable Mountains' and 'Jeremy Bird', (*FA2*, 106–8 and 110–12)

A passage from both versions of *This Is Thyself* (*FA2*, 109)

Two versions of a play called 'The Wood'

One version of a play entitled 'The Vacant Chair'

A draft scene-and-character-outline for a 3-Act play-version of the novel *Father Adam* (see next item) on two sides of one page, entitled *A New Commandment*, first title *Broken Commands* deleted.

Two manuscript versions of a full-length novel called *Father Adam*

A typescript of the novella *Father Adam*—to which Powys reduced the novel by deletion of a number of chapters—composed of partly top copy and partly carbon copy

The four countrymen who form a chorus commenting on the main action of the play must have been in Powys's mind for some time, for they appear in his writing as early as 1905 as the subject of 'Jeremy Bird' (above).[5] The short speeches uttered by the four countrymen in 'The Wood' become more highly developed conversations in the novel and the novella; both they and their wives figure substantially in some of the novel's discarded chapters—see extracts in *FA2*, 132–4 and 138–9.

The two plays to be considered in the context of the novella *Father Adam* are 'The Wood' and 'The Vacant Chair'. Put in a deceptively simple way, there are two Ams versions of the play: Ams 1, RD in a very-difficult-to-read hand, in four Acts, and Ams 2, a final large-neat-hand version in one Act of four scenes incorporating many changes. Each Ams is split up between the BC and the HRC. The 1st, 3rd and 4th Acts of the draft version are in 3 Ebs in the HRC, with Acts 1, 3 and 4 numbered on their respective covers. The 2nd Act, a play entitled 'The Vacant Chair', is in a BC Eb with *A New Commandment* (see above) and a RD of the play 'Father Adam'. In the final version the four Acts are changed to four Scenes and the original title 'The Hawk's Nest' is deleted and changed to 'The Wood/ a play in one Act', of which Scene 1 and part of Scene 2 are in 1 Eb in the BC and the rest of the play is in 2 Ebs in the HRC. At centre top Powys inscribed the front outer covers of the three Ebs: ~~*The Hawks nest*~~*/The Wood*, below that *T. F. Powys/ E. Chaldon/Dorchester,* below that *Miss E. M. Powys / 439 West 21st Street / New York City / U.S.A.*, and at the bottom *Miss K. Taylor/46 Olive Road/ London S. W. 19*. All three manuscripts concentrate on the history of the Owlsworth family; Keeper Owlsworth, his son Charley and his adopted daughter Mary Keyne, also known as Mary Owlsworth.

Powys wrote to Sylvia Townsend Warner on 18 June, 1927, 'The play about pheasants eggs was I think "The Hawks Nest"—And the man who broke the commandments "Father Adam."'[6] Powys had obviously forgotten not only that he changed the title of 'The Hawk's Nest' to 'The Wood', but also that in the final version he changed every mention of *hawk's nest* to *raven's nest*. Considering the great quantity of Powys's writing extant by 1927, this is not surprising.

Before being able to sort out the early versions, it was necessary to decipher 'The Vacant Chair' and the draft version of 'The Wood'. The whole task would have been less mind-contorting had Powys's Amss and Tmss not been scattered so blindly and indiscriminately around the world like so many pieces of meaningless paper, with even interpolated pages being mixed up between the two collections, sometimes with insufficient indications as to where exactly they belong. The second Act of the draft version appears to be missing. Yet more confusion arises because there are two attempts at the opening scene of Act I in the first HRC Eb, they are only separated by the word 'curtain' in the middle of a page, neither one is deleted, and there is absolutely no indication that the second one is a new beginning. In the first attempt, in which the opening scene is set in 'The wood', put very briefly, enter Mary Keyne and Charley Owlsworth, the latter dressed in soldier's uniform. There is no description of the two. They meet in the wood under the dead tree at the top of which Charley as a child hung his cap near a hawk's nest. Charley, who is going off to the war, tells Mary she must tell his father he's gone to Norfolk to buy pheasants' eggs, for the truth would break the old man's heart. Four countrymen arrive and conversation ensues. The lovers say goodbye and Mary goes home. Charley is joined in prayer by Mr Martin, who has not prayed for twenty years. Charley asks Mr Martin to look after Mary when his father dies, should he not return from the war. Mr Martin cannot, for he loves Mary. Charley says he would rather that Mary, if she were willing, would have Mr Martin 'than any young spark hereabout'. Charley leaves. The action is set in Enmore, accidentally called Tinclebury (the village in *The Market Bell*) just once. After the word 'curtain' in mid-page, the next scene is set in 'A wood'. Enter Mary Keyne in a white frock, and Charley Owlsworth—now dressed in his 'best holiday clothes'—miraculously back again. Both characters are introduced by means of a poetical description. They do not talk, the four countrymen appear very briefly, and there is an interpolation of a chorus of four countrywomen, labelled 'Extra piece Act II'. Neither version is deleted; one just follows the other. As the final version of the play has a similar poetical introduction with Mary dressed in a white frock and Charley in his best holiday clothes, I think one may presume that the second opening of the first scene was Powys's preferred one. The first-attempt conversation between Mary and Charley is retained, there being none in the second attempt, the 'Extra piece Act II' of four countrywomen's gossip is incorporated, and extra four-countrymen choruses are interpolated—all with various emendations and expansions.

In the BC Eb which contains 'A New Commandment' and the early version of the play 'Father Adam' (see above) there are thirty pages of the play 'The Vacant Chair'—first title 'The missing man' deleted, second title 'The only son' deleted. 'The Vacant Chair' begins in Powys's usual manner, with a list of characters followed by brief scene-settings for four acts, viz:

James Owlsworth
Mary Keynes ~~his daughter~~ his adopted daughter
Charles ~~John~~ his son missing in the great war.
Mr Robinson The new Squire of Enmore
Mrs Robinson his wife.
Country men.
Mr Punchin William Spokes
Walter Hinds Mr Hinks
Act I
The kitchen of the keeper's cottage.
Act II
The Village wall.
Act III
The stone Circle
Act IV
A deserted spot on the heath

Mrs Robinson never actually appears in play, novel or novella, Mr Hinks has not yet received his first name, and the only scene in 'The Vacant Chair' is the kitchen of the keeper's cottage. The village wall and the stone circle appear in neither play, but exist in the novel and the novella; the deserted spot on the heath is in 'The Wood' and the novel.

What is called Act I follows. There is an idyllic description of the cottage kitchen, Keeper Owlsworth and Mary. 'About this girl there breathes the divine goodness of innocence. She looks like a heath flower whose heart is love.' Tea is set for three, but Charley is 'late'. The keeper and Mary talk about Charley and about Mr Robinson's having had the wood felled, which has deeply upset the old keeper. Mr Martin brings Mary news of Charley's death but encourages her to hope. The four countrymen arrive and talk in the kitchen rather than at the village wall. As all this forms Act II of the early version of the play 'The Wood', one has to wonder why it begins like a new play, with a new description of Mary Keyne, who has already been described in Act I of 'The Wood' in the same words. There follow interpolations of choruses by the four countrymen, of choruses by the four countrywomen and of a scene in which Mr Neville tries to lead Mary away from the evil influence of the dead tree, between the evil Voice of which and himself there is a supernatural battle.

Act I of 'The Vacant Chair'—and there only is the one act—opens with the words, 'The season is winter', over which Powys has interpolated the words 'Seven months have passed'. Since this purports to be the opening of a new play, one might ask, 'Since when or what?' He has also interpolated the word 'now' in the opening sentence, so that it next reads, 'The season is now winter'. It would seem, therefore, that Powys wrote 'The Vacant Chair' first as a play in its own right, then at a later stage, by means of the interpolations, he adjusted the opening in order to use it as Act II of 'The Wood'. Whereas 'The Vacant Chair' certainly cannot be regarded as a finished play in itself—the ending is indeterminate—it does form a complete Act II for the draft version of 'The Wood'. The final version proves this conclusively, because the second of its four acts (or scenes, as they become), contains the substance of 'The Vacant Chair', including the interpolations. It begins in the same way (the italics being mine): 'Seven months have passed *since the first Act*. The season is now winter.' This important additional 'since the first Act' proves that 'The Vacant Chair' did indeed become the second Act of 'The Wood'. Less importantly, 'seven' is deleted and 'six' substituted.

At a later stage I found additional confirmation on the front cover of the BC Eb containing 'The Vacant Chair', on which Powys had written—as well as words connected with other items in the Eb—'The Hawk's Nest'. The writing is so faded and so faint that it can only just be made out, but 'The Hawk's Nest' was the deleted title of the HRC Ams final version of 'The Wood'. Powys must have added it after deciding to use 'The Vacant Chair' as Act II of 'The Hawk's Nest', before finally changing its title to 'The Wood'.

Powys has written 'Ch xxv' in the top margin at the beginning of the first opening scene of the draft version, but the contents have no connection with Chapter xxv in either version of the novel, nor with the corresponding Chapter xiv of the novella, in which there is in any case no Chapter xxv.

In the later Ams, which is 'A play in one Act', Powys crossed out the original four Acts and substituted four Scenes. Those things from the draft version which are dispensed with in the later version are also unused in the novel and novella, such as all scenes involving Mr Neville, all supernatural scenes, and the scene between Charley and Mr Martin.

The first Eb of the final version is in the BC and contains only the first Scene and part of the second Scene, in a large neat hand. There are fifty-four pages and a list of characters inside the front cover. The rest, in exercise books

II & III, is in the HRC, including, on both sides of a separate single sheet, a two-page scene-outline of the play 'Father Adam'.

Everything in the final version of the 'The Wood' goes into the full-length novel, where it takes equal place with the history of Father Adam, and Mary is called Eva.

The balance changes markedly in the Tms/Tccms (the novella), in which the Owlsworths recede into the background, much of the action is referred to briefly as being in the past and Charley becomes Eva's dead brother rather than her betrothed, leaving her free to bestow her heart upon Father Adam.

The Owlsworth components which remain in the novella are, briefly:

1 'A new Commandment I give unto you, that ye love one another.'

2 John Crew, Ralph Crew's father. In both versions of the play he is talked of as the good squire John Crew, now dead and replaced by the bad squire Mr Robinson.

3 Mr Martin—Father Adam's guide and confessor after Ralph Crew's death, and supporter of the love between Father Adam and Eva, as he is of that between Charley and Mary in the early version of the play.

4 Michael Owlsworth, keeper, who is in receipt of a pension because his son was killed in the war. He believes his son has gone to Norfolk to buy pheasants' eggs. When he dies he sighs peacefully.

5 Charley Owlsworth, Keeper Owlsworth's son, killed in the war.

6 Eva Owlsworth, his daughter, who is 'faithful to old Owlsworth', loving and possessed of domestic virtues. In the play she is Mary Keyne, also known as Mary Owlsworth, adopted daughter of the keeper.

7 Mr Robinson, the squire, who here would throw the sick old keeper out of his cottage, but in the play allows him to stay on.

8 Josiah Punchin, William Spokes, Walter Hinds, Jeremy Hinks, four countrymen, who lean on the ancient wall in the centre of the village, gossiping. In the play they gossip in the wood and in the keeper's kitchen.

There are some interesting differences between the two versions of 'The Wood', particularly concerning Mr Neville. Mr Martin appears as a good man in Act I of the draft version. He is deleted and changed to Mr Neville in Act II. On a loose page tipped in at the end of Act II is a conversation between Mary and Charley, not used elsewhere, concerning Mr Neville once having been a priest and leaving his village when his windows were stoned and broken because people didn't like his teaching—'love one another'—See *FA2*, p. 93: 'A new Commandment I give unto you, that ye love one another.' In Act II the four countrywomen say, 'If we listened to Mr Neville there be no pleasure in life.' Mr Neville is based on the outcast priest in Powys's autobiographical piece *This is Thyself* (*SEW*, lxxiii; complete, 325–67). He is deleted from the final version of 'The Wood'—with adjustments made in which other characters refer to him as 'the Parson' where necessary—but he is brought to fruition in Powys's novel *Mr. Tasker's Gods*, where he is cast out not only because he had kissed a girl, but also 'because he had tried and failed to defend the victim against the exploiter'. When he died, the people 'could never forgive or forget the way their late vicar had looked at them, and the way he forgave them their hatred.' Later, Powys was to express this theme in more humorous vein. In 'When Thou Wast Naked' (*Bottle's Path*) he writes of 'a babe, who was able to make all the fun of the world, even going so far, in his merriment, as to tell a man that he should love his neighbour'; and in 'The Only Penitent' (*Bottle's Path*) we read, 'There were few who knew Mr Hayhoe—with the exception perhaps of Mr Jar, the travelling tinker—who did not consider him both a fool and a simpleton … having only one idea in his life—to love all men.'

It should be well known by now that editing T. F. Powys can pose problems of punctuation, particularly the lack of indentation of paragraphs. However, this is a little less obvious in plays than in prose. In 'The Wood' many speeches are too short for paragraphing to be relevant and others are divided by stage directions. Where the speeches or the stage directions themselves are longer, some paragraphs fortunately end mid-line, leaving fewer choices to be made than in Powys's prose writings.

Powys's punctuation is unconventional; it follows natural speech rhythms.[7] To conventionalise it would often change its more subtle sense, so it is with some reluctance that I have added a minimum of commas where the meaning would be otherwise too ambiguous. I have generally left his characteristic longer sentences made up of two or more shorter ones separated by commas, the same-subject logic of which I find convincing.

Although the final version is written in a large clear hand, interpolations in pencil are very faint in my photocopy of the Ams, and some are squeezed in awkwardly; nevertheless, I hope and believe that I have managed to place them as Powys intended. However, I am doubtful about one later addition to the Ams. It is in thick ink within brackets—indicated in footnote 31 on p. 131. It reads clumsily and hurriedly and is a pedantic intrusion which does not let the play speak for itself. It is in the hand of Llewelyn Powys, whose editings date from summer 1919 to autumn 1920, the year when he returned from East Africa and stayed at the Weymouth address, where his father Rev. Charles

Powys, and his sister Gertrude, lived after leaving Montacute Vicarage.

Some of the many deletions have caused difficulties, partly because of their showing up only faintly in the photocopies. Shorter passages are crossed out by means of one, two or even three horizontal lines through each line of writing; longer ones are crossed through by vertical lines from top to bottom of the page, about half an inch apart. Both types of deletion-lines sometimes run over onto part of what should be un-deleted sections. In those places I have left the over-runs un-deleted.

I leave the last word—an important one—to Ian Robinson:

I wonder whether the stage directions telling us things we couldn't possibly know by looking at a performance may not just be TFP being simple-minded. He may have been thinking more of a reading text, or some sort of hybrid. You quote him as saying that the three plays would make a short book. The precedent is George Bernard Shaw, who certainly wanted his plays staged but then published them with stage directions sometimes much longer than the dialogue, that amount to a commentary and move the play in the direction of a novel. Shaw somewhere makes someone say *knee* for *née* which you couldn't get in stage performance. There's also Shakespeare. The demand for the quartos proves that Shakespeare was read as well as acted. ''To a strange hollow and confused noise they heavily vanish,' in *The Tempest*, is hardly a stage direction (what is a hollow noise and how do you heavily vanish?), more an appeal to the imagination of a reader. Alfred Hart noticed long ago that a number of Shakespeare plays, beginning with *Hamlet*, are too long for the 'two hours' traffic of the stage'.[8] It may well be that Shakespeare sometimes wrote two versions of his plays, one for the stage, one to be read. Two versions of *King Lear* survive; it makes sense to take the first quarto as (usually) the reading copy, the folio the acting text. It would be the find of the century if the reading version of *Macbeth* turned up: there is only the acting version.

NOTES FOR AFTERWORD

1 On 12 October 1920 Powys wrote to his sister Marian Powys in America, 'I am sending you a short country comedy, that there may possibly be an opening for.' and—on 14 October 1920—'I suppose I can do short country comedies like the one I send.' (*PJ* XII, 2000, 128, 130).

2 11 November 1920: 'I am trying at one more play called 'Blind Bartimæus'. I am only just making a start at it.'

16 November 1920: 'I have to copy out one more short country play. The three together would I suppose make a short book.'
24 November 1920: 'I am at present copying out "Blind Bartimæus" the last of the three plays.' (HRC)

The Ebs containing the final versions of the *Three Country Plays* are inscribed on the front covers, in Powys's hand, with their titles, Powys's address *T. F. Powys/E. Chaldon/Dorchester* near the top, *Miss E. M. Powys / 439 West 21st Street / New York City / U.S.A.* below, and *Miss K. Taylor/46 Olive Road/London S. W. 19* at the bottom.

3 For an account of Powys's various hands, and a folder of facsimiles of same, see *SEW*, xiii–xvi—or 'Editing T. F. Powys', by Elaine Mencher, *PJ* XVII 2007, 69–71, but the photocopy Ams samples on pp.78–86 are in black and white, reduced to 65% of their original size, and there is no Tms sample.

4 In a letter in the Sterling Library of London University, from Powys to Sir Louis Sterling, dated 15 March 1931, Powys tells the addressee, 'Mr Stirling', that *Mark Only* was written 'during the Summer and Autumn of 1922. ... The ground that it speaks of is the same ground that I step upon daily.'

5 Dated 1905 by Professor J. Lawrence Mitchell in *PJ* X (2000), 23.

6 BC. Powys's punctuation.

7 For Ian Robinson's account of Powys's punctuation see *The Market Bell*, first edition, pp. 284–87, and second edition, pp. 353–7.

8 Alfred Hart, *Shakespeare and the Homilies: And Other Pieces of Research into the Elizabethan Drama.*

BIBLIOGRAPHY

By T. F. Powys, editions used

Amos Lear, [novel], *Selected Early Works of T. F. Powys* as below.
'Blind Bartimaeus' [play], *The Powys Journal* XVI (2006), 121–72; Afterword, 173-7.
'The Candle and the Slow-Worm' [short story], *Fables* [short stories] (London: Chatto & Windus, 1929).
'Cottage Shadows' [novella], *Selected Early Works of T. F. Powys* as below.
'The Delectable Mountains' [seed-piece sketch], *Father Adam* [novella] as below.
'The Devil' [short story], *The House With the Echo* [short stories] (London: Chatto & Windus, 1928).
Father Adam [novella], second edition, (Denton: Brynmill, 2002).
'Father Adam' [play], *Selected Early Works of T. F. Powys* as below.
'Jeremy Bird' [seed-piece sketch], *Father Adam* as above.
Mark Only [novel] (London: Chatto & Windus 1924).
The Market Bell [novel], first edition (Gringley: Brynmill, 1991).
The Market Bell [novel], second edition (Bishopstone: Brynmill, 2006).
'The Midnight Hour' [short story], *Three Short Stories*, (Loughton: The Dud Noman Press, 1971).
Mockery Gap [novel] (London: Chatto & Windus 1925).
'Mrs Cern' [autobiography], *Selected Early Works of T. F. Powys* as below.
Mr. Tasker's Gods [novel] (London: Chatto & Windus 1924).

Mr. Weston's Good Wine [Novel] (London: The New Phoenix Library, Chatto & Windus 1950).
The Only Penitent, [long story] (London: Chatto & Windus 1931).
The Second Child [allegory; extracts], *Selected Early Works of T. F. Powys* as below.
Selected Early Works of T. F. Powys, edited with an Introduction and Notes by Elaine Mencher (Denton: Brynmill, 2003).
'This Is Thyself' [autobiographical], *Selected Early Works of T. F. Powys* as above.
'When Thou Wast Naked' [long story], *Bottle's Path* [stories] (London: Chatto & Windus 1946).

Criticism and Biography

Hart, Alfred: *Shakespeare and the Homilies: And Other Pieces of Research into the Elizabethan Drama* (Melbourne University Press, 1934).
Mencher, Elaine:
—— 'Blind Bartimaeus': Afterword, *The Powys Journal* XVI, 2006, 173–7.
—— 'Editing T. F. Powys', with photocopy samples of T. F. Powys manuscripts, *The Powys Journal* XVII (2007), 78–86.
—— 'The Genesis of *Father Adam*', *Father Adam*, second edition (Denton: Brynmill, 2002), 105–140.
Mitchell, J. Lawrence:
—— '*Commentary* on works by TFP', *The Powys Journal* X (2000), 20–24.
Pouillard, Michel:
—— 'T. F. Powys and the Theatre', *The Powys Review* 5 (1980), 45–6.
Powys, T. F.:
—— 'Why I Have Given Up Writing', *John O'London's Weekly and Outlook*, October 23rd 1936. Vol. XXXVI.
Robinson, Ian:
—— On T. F. Powys's punctuation: *The Market Bell*, first edition, pp. 284–7, and *The Market Bell*, second edition, pp. 353–7.

ACKNOWLEDGEMENTS

I would like to thank Ian Robinson and Barrie Mencher for proof-reading, Ian Robinson for suggestions—see, in particular, the last paragraph of the Afterword—and Anna Chen of the HRC for fielding manuscript queries. My thanks go retrospectively to E. E. Bissell for the generous loan of his T. F. Powys unpublished manuscripts and typescripts, photocopies of which I am still using today, including parts of both manuscript versions of 'The Wood'. I am indebted to the Harry Ransom Research Center, The University of Texas at Austin, for the use of the remaining parts of the two versions.

Elaine Mencher

LOUISE DE BRUIN

'Begin at the Door': in search of Vera Stacey Wainwright

On my first walks in Mappowder with Gerard Casey, Lucy Penny's son-in-law, Gerard showed me the Powysian landmarks: Heaven's Gate, Lucy's Gate, Theodore's Walk, the Lodge, Theodore's grave, the little brook T. F. Powys had named the Oxus, and many others. One morning he stopped in front of one of Mappowder's oldest cottages, and asked me to have a look inside the porch. I did, and saw above the door a small wooden panel with the name 'Mockery-Gap', surrounded by little toy-like figures, delicately painted and happy-looking. 'That used to be Vera's cottage, a good friend of Theodore's', Gerard said. 'She was one of the very few who towards the end of his life Theodore did not mind accompanying him on his walks, so much so that even Lucy on occasion was a bit jealous of her.'

That afternoon, after tea in the garden, Gerard opened an ochre-coloured booklet with a picture of a strange mask on the cover, said solemnly, 'This is one of Vera's poems', and read:

From the Dark Room

From the dark room I opened the door
And was amazed
To see the kitchen ablaze.
The dawn sunlight
Shone strong through the skylight
Onto things ordinary and poor.
They stood in strange transfiguration:
And the packet of Lux was singing
It seemed to itself in bliss:
'O Lux perpetualis!'

Gerard's reading had the probably desired effect. I was impressed, and wanted to know more about this Vera who was not only an artist with the boldness to change the name of her cottage from Meadow View to Mockery Gap, but could also make Lucy jealous and write an exquisite poem about a simple packet of washing powder. When I left Mappowder that dry summer of 1976 Gerard gave me a copy of Vera's poems to which I would regularly return over the years, each time enchanted. But for a long time I didn't find out much more about the poet than the few biographical facts given in a note at the end of the little book.

Some years later, after Mary Casey, Gerard's wife, had died and The Enitharmon Press brought out posthumously a first small volume of her poetry, *Full Circle*, I met Vera again, and again through a poem:

Mockery Gap

for Vera ...

once this was the house of an elf-child
the little lady who kept frail life-hold
with her paints and dyed wool-balls
flowers by the walls and bird calls

I shall not open the door again
to find her alone with her loom
and a fire too low to burn too low to go out
the Russian toys and wings at the window-pane

was it this year she caught me with changeling hands
clung as a bat clings—darling I love you so
her cold eyes clear as pools of rain
in elf-land whence she came

... who died 29.10.67

And then one day I came to live in Mappowder. No more excuses now. I started to question people in the village who had known Vera, went through Mary's journals and Lucy's diaries, talked to Gerard again, made an appointment with Gregory Stevens Cox whose father James had founded with his wife The Toucan Press which had first published

Poems and Masks (Poems by Vera Wainwright, Masks by Austin O. Spare; Guernsey, 1968), asked Professor J. L. Mitchell what he could tell me, came by a stroke of luck across Vera's only surviving relation in Australia and was finally able to piece some fragments of her life together. But here first, is the short autobiography that James Stevens Cox had asked her to write.

I was born in London in 1893. Went to Australia when I was two —where my Father died.

From the age of seven until twenty-one my home was in a then remote and unspoilt Surrey village. My mother remarried when I was about twelve. Until then a succession of governesses had given me a smattering of education but at this age I was sent to a Catholic Convent school in Sussex. I subsequently fell ill there and returned home for a year, with periodic visits to London for treatment for spinal curvature. Finally I spent a short time at a Catholic Convent school in London.

About 1913 I met in London Charles Edward Laurence, novelist & reader at John Murray's, and retained his friendship until his death in 1940. In the *Times* obituary he was referred to as 'one of the best known and best loved man of letters in London'.

Aged twenty-one I took a cottage near Haslemere but left it later for rooms in Coldharbour, near Leith-hill, where, for a time, I kept the Tower open to visitors.

Then, knapsack on back, rambled on the Sussex Downs. Sent a poem to Victor Neuburg at Steyning and later met him there.

Soon after World War I, I went to Paris to study at La Grande Chaumière and also to have private lessons with the sculptor Louis Ovry & accompanied him and his family to Normandy where I first met Robert Sherard.

Later I studied painting with a Corsican professional in Nice and painted, under his guidance, in Corsica, Algeria and Morocco.

Visited les Eyzies, Dordogne, stayed at the same hotel as the Abbé Breuil & other professors of pre-history.

Travelled also in Spain & was in Madrid on the night the King abdicated.

At Avignon, France, I met the sculptor Jean Pierre Gras, well known in that city for his outstanding work.

Back in England Walter de la Mare was not only a kind and generous friend but one who gave much encouragement over my poems & who published a sonnet in his anthology *Love*, and reprinted in this volume [*Poems and Masks*].

I met also in London E. H. Visiak, authority on Milton, and the poets Henry Savage & Louis McQuilland. Algernon Blackwood was a delightful visitor when I stayed in Chelsea.

During World War II Victor Neuburg gave me an introduction to Austin O. Spare; I am hoping to write my memoirs of him.

In 1927 I had the great happiness of meeting the Powys family & this has considerably enriched my life.

I have had a few poems published in periodicals & have written some travel sketches & one novel — these as yet unpublished.

FINIS!

Beneath these autobiographical notes Vera had written: 'Dear Mr Stevens Cox, can you make anything worthwhile of enclosed? There were other "activities" such as my joining (when about 20 years old) a Society for the Protection of the Public against the Police—of which Bernard Shaw was a member! However, in view of the recent murder of the 3 policemen [the Shepherd's Bush Murders, 12 August 1966], this is for your ears alone. Am much "under the weather" with ear trouble but hope that what I have written will be of some use. Best wishes, Vera Wainwright'.

When I first read this brief autobiography, printed as a biographical note in the third person singular by Stevens Cox at the end of *Poems and Masks*, I thought, 'why does he indulge in all this name-dropping; doesn't her poetry speak for itself, doesn't it show she was a remarkable woman in her own right?' After his son Gregory had given me a photocopy of Vera's typescript, I knew I had been unfair to his father, that it was Vera herself who had written like this. It made me sad—such lack of self-confidence, such what we now would call 'groupie' behaviour. Later, I would find out how lonely and alone she was most of the time and come to realise that this was probably one of her ways of coping; keeping the light of her life burning by searching out other, seemingly stronger, lights.

A portrait of Vera by the artist Henry Lawrence (exh. 1880–1907) shows a rather pretty, shy young woman with a beautiful mass of dark hair, well-shaped eyebrows, straight nose and brown eyes reminding me somewhat of Lucy Penny as a young woman. She came from a well-to-do family: her father had gone out to western Australia to manage the family business—large warehouses and other business interests in the town of Geraldton. (His son Mervyn Beauchamp, slightly younger than Vera, who was born back in England after their father's death at the early age of thirty-five, would later move to Australia too.) Her mother's maiden name was Barclay and she was—according to one of her friends—related to the Barclays of the Bank. Vera had her own income all her life, in part from real estate in London, and also, as she noted in a letter to Austin Spare, 'my own relations are almost too generous to me'. At her death she left a considerable sum of money to her brother, to the surprise of most Mappowder villagers since she had lived such a simple life. That she never married was—according to her brother—because of her spinal problems. But what do brothers really know?

Was it chance, choice, or circumstances that made her put her knapsack on her back and set out alone? In her poem, 'The Rolling Stone', she wrote,

> A rolling stone,
> I gather no moss.
> Oh, come with me
> Where all is loss.
>
> I wear no crown,
> I carry no cross,
> Oh, come with me
> Where all is loss.
>
> Bare, bare, bereft, bereft
> I roll along. Nor cliff nor cleft
> Stay my career.
> I do not belong—

Nor there nor here.
I have no home
And I gather no moss
Nor brake nor bone …
You will not come?
I travel alone—
Ever alone—the rolling stone.

And in one of her letters to Spare she referred to her 'gypsy nature'. Before her arrival in Mappowder she had lived in many more places, both in the United Kingdom and abroad, than she had mentioned in her autobiographical note: Cornwall, Devon, Dorset, Alessio, Bandol, to name but a few. Some of these places she had chosen because of her ill-health (many were the periods she spent in hospitals and nursing-homes for the various illnesses connected with her spinal curvature, her weak lungs and, later in life, tinnitus), some to see friends or to paint.

Glimpses of what Vera's life was like before she came to live in Mappowder can best be caught from her recollections of the journalist, biographer and novelist Robert Harborough Sherard (1861–1943) whom she met around 1922, and from her letters to the artist, writer and occultist Austin Osman Spare (1886–1956). But John Cowper Powys, to whom Vera devoted a poem, also adds a few snippets of information, mainly in his diary kept during the time he lived in Dorset after his return from the USA. (Phyllis Playter met Vera regularly, visiting her both in hospital in Dorchester and in Cerne Abbas where Vera then lived.) The writer Algernon Blackwood's (1869–1951) letters to her, now in the British Library, and T. F. Powys's letters, also in the British Library, have proven of little interest in this respect, although on 25 December 1935 Theodore wrote that she is 'not one of the proud ones I am glad to say to want to be set up too high—There is danger there.' One also learns that it was Vera who sent T. F. Powys a book by Kierkegaard, of whom he had never heard. Walter de la Mare (1873–1956), another of her pen-friends, wrote to her mainly about her poetry. In her own words: 'To my friend, Walter de la Mare, I owe a great debt of gratitude for his unfailing encouragement and criticism.' It was her sonnet 'Then Waits the Heart' that de la Mare published in his anthology *Love*.

Then Waits the Heart

When we are older and the hidden fires
Burn not so brightly, burn low but are not extinguished;
The flames have flickered but have not relinquished
Their impulse utterly; when young desires,
—Whose tender music had robbed the angel choirs—
Are spent; when no more, no more can be distinguished
From quiet sorrow the sword-thrusts that so anguished
Us; Oh, when all ecstasied Love expires:

Then waits the heart, waits, inarticulate, dumb,
Cowled like a monk, secretive, sad, alone,
Filled with far meditation ... Marks the hour,
Perchance, when One, compassionate, should come.
—As back to an abandoned nest had flown
The bird, all heedless of its fading bower.

Finally, there is Steffi Grant's Introduction to *Zos Speaks! Encounters with Austin Osman Spare* (1998, dedicated to Vera), though it is somewhat difficult to recognise Vera in the rather condescending account she gives of her.

Vera's reminiscences of Robert Sherard were published in several parts in *The Literary Repository* (between 1966 and 1968). She first met Sherard, when she was not quite thirty and he nearing sixty, in a bookshop in Vernon-sur-Eure in Normandy. They quickly discovered a mutual interest in natural history, which would form the basis of their friendship. Together they studied many species: hornets, butterflies, beetles, birds, stray dogs, beggars and other human beings. They saw quite a lot of each other in the first years after their meeting; in Vernon, in Bandol, Alessio and Nice, where Vera had gone to nurse a sick friend, the daughter of Dostoevsky (Lyubov, 1869–1926)—a fact that later would greatly impress John Cowper Powys. In those days Sherard was a regular contributor to *The Caterer*, so they had fun together in Nice looking at the menu-cards posted outside the restaurants. Once, at a tea shop, they found to their great amusement on a menu-card written for the benefit of English visitors 'Bums 6d'. Later they would write to each other frequently and regularly. Vera quotes a lot from Sherard's letters, which give a fascinating and moving picture of this one-time friend (and first biographer) of Oscar Wilde. The last words Sherard would write to her two years before his death were: 'I am very glad we met upon this earth'.

It was, as Vera wrote herself, the poet and writer Victor Neuburg (1883–1940) who gave her an introduction to Austin Osman Spare. Neuburg was already very ill by then and would die shortly afterwards. Among the many young poets and writers to whom he had stood literary godfather, first by giving them a chance in his 'Poet's Corner' in the *Sunday Referee*, and later in his magazine *Comment*, were Dylan Thomas, Pamela Hansford Johnson, David Gascoyne and Francis Berry. Vera herself had two of her short stories published in *Comment*.

Not long after her first meetings with Spare, Vera moved from Chelsea to a rented cottage in Helford, Cornwall, and so began an exchange of letters (published in *Art & Letter: Word & Sign*, 2003). Unfortunately, the only part of the correspondence that survives are Vera's letters from February 1943 till February 1946. Although certainly not of great literary interest they throw a fascinating light on their friendship during the later war years. From these letters Vera emerges as a strong-willed and kind woman, albeit a bit fussy at times. There is a lot about the domestic side of life (mattresses, bed linen, furniture, coal and the size of macaroni crop up regularly), money and health matters (Spare like Vera had his share of ill-health), but also about art, both Vera's and Spare's. After his flat had been bombed, Vera proposed they take an apartment together in London. It has been suggested she was in love with him, but to me this seems doubtful. I have the feeling she was true to herself when she wrote to him in August 1944: 'Supposing it does not go beyond "very close friendship", will you still find that worth having?' In other letters she wrote: 'Human relations are mysterious. With you I have been dynamic because strongly impelled.' And, 'Friendship, Love, Sex—big subjects really—& looked at differently by women & men (very often). Later we may have some interesting conversations ... .' Whatever the truth, she certainly invited him to come and stay with her in Pear Tree Cottage in Helford as he finally did on 23 March 1944, his fare paid in advance by Vera. It was there that they first discussed Spare's idea for a monthly limited subscribers' magazine of poetry and art. He would design several lay-outs for this project (see Vera Wainwright and Austin O. Spare, *The Poetry and Art*), but the magazine never saw the light of day.

A few weeks later Spare left again with a cheque for £50 from Vera as rent for their future apartment in London. Many more cheques would follow over the next few years, although in the meantime he had moved in with his old sweetheart Ada Millicent Paine. Vera had gone to a little house near Liskeard to paint the miners' cottages in the area by the time she found out Spare had 'blown' the money. She did not hesitate to take him to task for this. Spare eventually would honour his debt in his own way: shortly after his first post-war exhibition, held at the Archer Gallery in London, he sent her a cheque for £10 and in his Will he left her ten pictures after first having proposed to make her the sole beneficiary of his Will—a proposal Vera refused.

How their friendship continued after February 1946 is difficult to know, but in a short letter that did survive, dated 20 December 1954, Vera writes:

> Dearest Austin,
> [...] Thinking of you rather deeply, I conclude that you are on the threshold of saint-hood but have not yet crossed it! You still face darkness often, but you could turn towards light—as it is there at your elbow. You could be quite a wonderful person, but to change the metaphor—there is still a little devil at your coat-tail!
> With love,
> Vera

* * * *

In a letter to Vera of 30 March 1926 T. F. Powys remarked that he had 'hoped that *Innocent Birds* would make a convert, and now that it has I am content', so it was probably after a fan letter from Vera and the following correspondence that in 1927 a first meeting was arranged.

Thus, when Violet Powys found her the Mappowder cottage in 1946 or '47, Vera had known Theodore and Violet for about twenty years. She was now in her fifties, and in her poem Mary Casey caught the essential nature of the 'tiny wan Walter de la Mare figure' (Mary's description in her Journal). This much was later confirmed by those in Mappowder who remembered her and had known her for many years.

'The sun never entered the low north-facing sitting-room, but her presence gave radiance to its dimness', her friend, the historian Barbara Kerr, would write in a short obituary. Another friend, this one in the village, told me, 'her house was plain and clean with lots of books and pictures. I would cook for Vera who was a vegetarian, because she would not cook for herself. She bought the land on the Green where there was a sort of copse where gypsies used to stay because she didn't want neighbours.' According to another, 'When she went for a walk (which was most often with Mr Powys) she used to carry a pen-knife with some sort of antidote against snakes strapped to her wrist. She reminded me a bit of Miss Katie [Powys], but then of course much more feminine. She was somewhat bent like Miss Katie, carrying a stick. Some of the village children were afraid of her and called her a witch.' That may be forgivable, because she was unusual by the village standards of those days, dressed in 'a kind of artistic clothes, home-made skirts and shawls, both woven by herself on her own loom'. Most children, however, she put effortlessly at ease and they loved being in her cottage where on occasion she would settle them down at a small table with real tea in the pot of a tiny tea-set.

One of the two downstairs rooms she turned into a shop to sell her hand-woven ties, shawls, scarves, etc. and her own paintings and water-colours. In the spring the grass close to the cottage on the Hammond Street side where the children waited for the school bus was ablaze with daffodils, and coconut halves were always strung up in winter for the birds. To join Theodore for his walks she would probably have taken the foot-path that went from the side of her house to the gate opposite the Lodge and it was on those walks that she took mental note of some of Theodore's casual remarks which once back home she would write down: there are about twenty of them (now in the British Library)—a rare testimony of T. F. Powys's thoughts during the last years of his life. That Powys's thinking had not changed much since he had stopped writing may be clear from the following:

> Walk with Th. in the hayfield. He said that the modern bales of hay had something unclean about them.—27 June 1947
>
> Th. told me that a woman talking to Violet on the subject of cleaning the house had said that one should 'begin at the door', and it struck him as a very good title for a story: 'Begin at the Door'.—November 1947
>
> A very blowy late afternoon, with clouds and clear sky spaces. Walked to meet Theodore on the Plush road and on our return walk, we looked over to the distant Shaftesbury hill, the houses standing out in the bright sunlight, with the shadowy valley between, and Theodore said that Bunyan's Celestial City must have appeared to him like that.—3 August 1949
>
> Th. suggested that the third God was 'God the Goblin' (in place of the Holy Ghost).
>
> It was one of the mildest November days Th. remembers. Violet's tobacco plants had a few flowers against the grey wall of the Lodge. Crimson yew berries were strewn on the road near the churchyard. We looked at the bare ash and at the oak still full of golden brown foliage, and I said: 'It seems only a little while ago that we were discussing whether the ash or the oak had come into leaf first'. Th. made an almost startled movement. 'Yes', he said, 'it does. It only shows', he continued half to himself, 'with life so short how little our worries matter.'
>
> On one of my last walks with him, Th. picked some hog-weed, crushing the seed in his hand and saying how one felt the *animal* beneath the plant.

Until ill-health confined her within the walls of Mockery Gap and its garden Vera continued to travel abroad and in England. During her absences she often lent or rented her cottage to friends or friends of friends. Mark Holloway and Joan Lamburn, friends of Alyse Gregory, came to stay, together and separately. So did Louis Wilkinson. In 1951

Joan would buy Dove Cottage in nearby Hazelbury Bryan and later become Louis Wilkinson's fourth wife before her sudden death in 1957, leaving Alyse Gregory who had just bought a house in Hazelbury Bryan to be near her so utterly bewildered and lost that she accepted—rather too quickly maybe—an invitation to go and live in Devon.

When Vera was at home friends and acquaintances were always welcome too: many Powyses and Powys friends visited; among them Katie and Phyllis who had first met Vera in 1934 at Theodore's. Lucy also became a good friend. Her diary often mentions Vera: 'Called on Vera', 'Vera called on me', 'Last night I saw Vera's picture made in Cornwall', 'Walked with Vera to Shortwood', 'Vera sat with me in the garden and talked of dead doctors helping to heal the living!', 'Said goodbye to Vera who goes to Corsica on Monday' (12 June 1954), 'Vera had 4 tits at her coconuts: 2 great tits and 2 blue tits' (12 Jan 1955), 'Went to see Vera who is soon going to Algiers. She is not very well' (9 Aug 1955), 'Took Will's picture to Vera to look at. She goes into Sherborne Hospital tomorrow' (27 Sept 1955).

In 1957 Vera thought of moving to Cornwall permanently. In a letter of 13 February 1957 Lucy wrote to Mary, 'Vera says unless she can sell her house here by October she will have to forfeit the deposit on the Cornish one.' This might have happened, because she returned to Mappowder later that month and told Lucy some time afterwards that she had entirely changed her mind about selling Mockery Gap.

Vera's health continued to decline. By August 1967 she was in bed with bad bronchitis; it is from now on that Lucy organised her care with the assistance of Vera's devoted helpers Bessie Trevett and her daughter Eileen, Mrs Ayres, Kathleen Vallence and a few others. On 25 October 1967, after a bad fall, she was taken to Portland Hospital where she died on Sunday 29 October, Mrs Ayres by her side. (Afterwards Vera's brother sent a letter from Australia with his thanks and a cheque to Mrs Ayres for the help she had given.) She was cremated at Weymouth crematorium on 6 November (a beautiful day, according to Lucy's diary) and her ashes were scattered as stipulated in her Will. Two days later two men from Lloyds Bank, the executor and trustee of her Will, came to have a look at her cottage and to lunch with

Lucy; shortly afterwards her home of twenty years was emptied so quickly and thoroughly that even Lucy, who had wanted to retrieve the portrait Vera had begun of Mary in June 1964, was taken by surprise: everything had disappeared. According to the second codicil to her Will made in April 1947 in Mappowder, Captain John Lennard, a young man (he was born *c.*1914) when Vera first befriended him and whom she looked upon as a kind of son, was the sole beneficiary of her papers, books, pictures and so on, with the exception of an etching 'Hangmans House, Tours' by Whistler which she had bequeathed to the British Museum and a beautiful little painting by her friend the 'Corsican professional', O. Madrigale, called 'Maisons de Erbalanga' that was left to Lucy. (Some of her papers turned up in an auction some years ago, among them six previously unpublished short stories—several very short indeed, more like vignettes—and eight poems that had not been included in *Poems and Masks.*) Of her other earthly belongings all that remains of Vera in Mappowder now are a few keepsakes, a few photographs and some paintings that still hang on the walls in several cottages and in the church.

Although Vera was very committed to her painting, I find the pictures I have seen pleasant to look at, but not much more. When chance brought me in contact with Vera's niece in Australia I not only hoped that she would still have the many letters Vera had faithfully sent her brother over the years, but also that I would be able to change my opinion, but no, although the few landscape paintings by Vera her brother possessed are definitely among the better ones. (The letters had been destroyed.)

Vera was, in her own words, an out-of-doors painter, but often sickly and inclined to feel the cold there were long periods when she did not paint at all. On 8 January 1946 she wrote to Spare:

> Some one showed a few of my paintings to a (London) Gallery the other day & they turned them down because they said technique was not up to standard. Do you agree? I get rather discouraged sometimes.

And in February 1946: 'If I were a great draftsman like yourself, I should indeed work indoors! That is, if I, like you, had much to express.' What Spare thought exactly of her work, is not known, although he was always encouraging.

It is as the author of a slim volume of poems that Vera's name comes up when one looks for her on the internet, and—for better and for worse—always connected to Spare. Vera herself was the one who came up with the original idea for a collaboration between them:

> I might, however, say that few, too, jump to conclusions 'as I never suggested or wished for, nice, mild, kindly Edwardian' illustrations!!! Also, in my first letter, I said that the illustrations need not illustrate the poems—(or something equivalent). I admit that I somewhat retracted this statement by suggesting a spiritual harmony. [...] If you still wish to go on with it now, you'd better do so with a free hand. I'm not anti-bold & I am not easily shocked. [...] Of course you will share in the sales. I won't agree otherwise. You really ought to have it all—as your work will be what is admired. (2 February 1946)

And three days later:

> You once said that you were not keen to have your work reproduced (printed) & I understand what you mean. But, for example, there is a head—Pan—in that small book I had from you that I would rather like to have as a frontispiece to my poems!—when I have enough of these ready. In fact, it would be very splendid if there could be several of your drawings. (But I think the Public would be so keen on your work that they would overlook my poems.) All the same, I don't see why, if the idea appealed to you, this plan of a small volume should not take form.

Followed on 9 February 1946 by:

> This about our book (—I will write in answer to your kind letter & sketch a little later.)
>
> I am glad you are willing and shall be interested to see the 'rough conception of the idea'.
>
> My poems, as you will see, are slight, but they have been approved by reliable critics. But they have nothing ultra-modern about them

> & I don't personally feel that ultra-modern illustrative decorations would be in harmony!
>
> I do not want the book (for my part) to sell by 'sensational means', I'd rather abandon the idea. So you see, we don't agree here! The poems I send you (seven) are roughly of two kinds—carefully worked out sonnet & the others which are almost spontaneous. These latter, I feel, are easier to illustrate—if you can get into their mood—a little haunting. I would have a few more—making in all about a dozen. Therefore your 10 illustrations would be splendid. Because of shortage of paper, it may at first be a little difficult to find a publisher—but eventually we should be successful, I think … I will certainly do as you suggest & send you 10/– for 5 weeks.

Why the project then stalled (Spare sent her several sets of designs for the volume) is a mystery since no further letters survive. But twenty-two years later, in 1968, The Toucan Press finally published *Poems and Masks* with twenty-seven poems by Vera and five 'masks' by Spare. In the same year a second edition came out in the USA with an Introduction lovingly written by her goddaughter Stacey Biswas Day in which she quotes from one of Vera's letters to her, 'The greatest "sinners" are sometimes those who are the most understanding. It is true, in a sense, that we all wear a mask'. Sadly, for both Vera and Spare, the two small volumes came out posthumously. That *Poems and Masks* has seen five reprints to date (the latest in 2007), is proof of the spell this curious marriage of 'Word & Sign', the name they had chosen for the monthly magazine they had hoped to start in 1944, still casts.

Walter de la Mare wrote to her about one of her poems (impossible to know which one): 'I treasure that last poem. However well you write them they always appear to have "come", and I believe that is the secret, although of course one delights in exquisite and conscious finish.' Of 'The Straw' he said, it 'is a gem, its mouse a little angel. It is beautifully woven together and brimming over with meaning.'

The Straw

I am that straw
That broke the camel's back.
The straw that could not save
A man from sinking to his grave.

Yet I can
(So it goes,)
Tell the way
The wind blows …
I only ask to lie
Within the harvest field
—Forgotten in the carrying
Of that bright, homeward corn—
Till the time the moon has risen
And the owl calls long, forlorn,
Then the scurrying, whiskered mouse
Makes sortie from its prison.

It has a thousand fears,
And pauses as it peers.
The owl calls long, forlorn.
The mouse lifts its trembling paw,
Holds me within the wind:
'Which way, which way, O Straw?'

And of yet another one, 'The poem is a little masterpiece—little in the sense of its exquisite condensation. It is new and fresh and lovely in idea, feeling, expression and in detail … .' I like to think de la Mare is referring to 'The Poker':

The Poker

Hour after hour
I stand with my small poker face
As though I were in dire disgrace.

Then am I seized and in red coal
Am rudely thrust body and soul.
My sufferings none shall console.

But it could also have been:

So did it most swiftly pass

So did it most swiftly pass—
The shadow of a bird's wing on the grass,
Greying the colour, saddening it
For that brief second; then relit,
The bird had gone;
The grass with sunlight shone …
Was the bird aware,
Speeding onward through the air?
Was the grass dismayed
By so small and dear a shade?

Photographs of Vera Wainwright are reproduced on earlier pages:
Vera Wainwright as a young woman. (page 11)
Vera Wainwright in front of her Cottage Mockery Gap. (page 66)

ACKNOWLEDGEMENTS

For their kind and generous help I want to thank Eileen White and her late husband Stan, the late Kathleen Vallence, Vera's niece April Parks, A. R. Naylor, Professor J. L. Mitchell, Gregory Stevens Cox, Roger Peers, Rita Taylor, Peter J. Foss and Judith Ravenscroft.

WORKS CITED

Unpublished Papers

Vera Wainwright papers in The British Library (Record Reference: Add MS 54330).

Typescript of Vera Wainwright's autobiographical note, a photocopy of which was provided by Gregory Stevens Cox.

Mary Casey's journals.

Lucy Penny's diaries and letters to her daughter Mary Casey.

Copies of Vera Wainwright's Will and codicils.

Published materials

Ashley, Mike, *Starlight Man: The Extraordinary Life of Algernon Blackwood* (London: Constable, 2001): many letters from Blackwood to Wainwright quoted.

Boulton, John, 'Evening for T. F. Powys', *Notes and Queries*, 1972 19(9): 338–40.

Dictionary of British Artists, Vol. 5 (Antique Collectors' Club, 1990).

Fuller, Jean Overton, *The Magical Dilemma of Victor Neuburg* (Oxford: Mandrake Press, 2005).

Grant, Kenneth and Steffi, *Zos Speaks! Encounters with Austin Osman Spare* (London: Fulgur, 1998).

Holloway, Mark, 'With T. F. Powys in Mappowder', *Recollections of the Powys Brothers*, Belinda Humfrey ed. (London: Peter Owen, 1980), 149–63.

Kerr, Barbara, obituary of Vera Wainwright (undated & unattributed cutting).

Powys, John Cowper, *The Dorset Year: The Diary of John Cowper Powys June 1934–July 1935*, Morine Krisdóttir and Roger Peers eds. (Kilmersdon: Powys Press, 1998).

Scutt, Theodora Gay, *A Cuckoo in the Powys Nest: A Memoir* (Denton Harleston: Brynmill, 2000).

Spare, Austin O., & Vera Wainwright, *Art & Letter: Word & Sign* (I.H.O. Books, 2003).

Spare, Austin O, *Drawings by Austin O. Spare for V.S.W.* (Thame: I.H.O. Books, 2007).

Wainwright, Vera, 'Robert Harborough Sherard: Reminiscences', Parts 1 to 4, *The Literary Repository* (1966–1968).

Wainwright, Vera & Austin O. Spare, *Poems and Masks* (Guernsey: The Toucan Press, 1968).

Wainwright, Vera, *The Poetry & Art, Vera Wainwright and Austin O. Spare* (no colophon, presumably I.H.O. Books).

Wainwright, Vera & Austin O. Spare, *Poems and Masks, Vera Wainwright and Austin O. Spare* (no colophon, presumably I.H.O. Books).

Whistler, Theresa, *Imagination of the Heart: The Life of Walter de la Mare* (London: Duckworth, 1993). (No mention of Vera Wainwright.)

White, Eileen, *Memories of Mappowder* (privately printed, 2008).

RICHARD MAXWELL

The Iron Bar: a debt revisited

In *The Powys Journal* xvi (2006), I published an essay, 'A Game of Yes and No: Childhood and Apocalypse in *Porius*', in which I pointed out several episodes in novels by John Cowper Powys that had their source in Sir Walter Scott's 'Lay of the Last Minstrel'. A version of this essay now forms part of the concluding chapter of my book *The Historical Novel in Europe, 1650–1950* (Maxwell 2009, 260–73). In both versions I assumed that Powys was not merely impressed by Scott's poem, but that certain passages had been imprinted on his mind for life. Among these were the description of the knight digging up the Wizard with an iron bar; in a weird half-life the Wizard yields up to him a magic book which gets him through the rest of the story. That iron bar reappears in *A Glastonbury Romance*, where it is associated with Owen Evans's sadism, and in *Porius*, where it is associated with freeing the wizard himself, Merlin, from an enchantment that's tantamount to being buried.

I now wonder whether Powys's memory of Scott had not been supported by another iron bar, in a case of duplicate or mediated influence. Recently I have been reading W. Harrison Ainsworth's *Jack Sheppard* (1839), a lurid historical tale that recounts the criminal exploits of a formidable yet hapless youth, based on the historical figure of that name who was hanged at Tyburn in 1724, at the age of 22. Ainsworth's protagonist is hapless in that he is convicted for many crimes that he did not commit, being regularly tipped off or turned in by his rival, accomplice and nemesis Jonathan Wild; he is formidable in that, whatever the jail, he always makes his escape.

For Scott, the iron bar is primarily an implement, but for Ainsworth its first function is the securing of the prisoner:

> In consequence of Jack Sheppard's desperate character, it was

> judged expedient by the keeper of the New Prison to load him with fetters of unusual weight, and to place him in a cell which, from its strength and security, was called the Newgate Ward. The ward in which he was confined, was about six yards in length, and three in width, and in height, might be about twelve feet. The windows which were about nine feet from the floor, had no glass; but were secured by thick iron bars, and an oaken beam. Along the floor ran an iron bar to which Jack's chain was attached, so that he could move along it from one end of the chamber to the other. (Ainsworth, ch. 4)

The third and last volume of the novel is subtitled 'The Prison Breaker' and recounts in detail Jack's escape from Newgate. Chapter 17 is entitled 'The Iron Bar':

> Having worked thus for another quarter of an hour without being sensible of fatigue though he was half stifled by the clouds of dust which his exertions raised, he had made a hole about three feet wide, and six high, and uncovered the iron bar. Grasping it firmly with both hands, he quickly wrenched it from the stones in which it was mortised, and leapt to the ground. On examination it proved to be a flat bar of iron, nearly a yard in length, and more than an inch square. 'A capital instrument for my purpose,' thought Jack, shouldering it, 'and worth all the trouble I have had in procuring it.'

In order to escape, Jack must thus first dislodge the iron bar itself; this is accomplished by the virtual demolition of the room in which he finds himself locked. It is a wonder that the roof does not collapse and bury him. He then uses the loosed iron bar as a weapon with the help of which he proceeds to smash and pry his way out of prison. We cheer him on. He merely wants to attend his dear mother's funeral.

This episode is interesting for several reasons. The iron bar that held him prisoner is transformed into an instrument of escape. We are glad when Jack gets the use of it. Yet, while this episode has its redeeming aspects (the transformation of the bar from symbol of prison to means of release, the engaging humanity lying behind Jack's break for freedom), Powys himself, in the *Autobiography,* associates Ainsworth with violence in his very prose style:

> But at school I used to devour voraciously ... the works of

> Harrison Ainsworth. These lurid tales—*Herne the Hunter*, *The Tower of London*, *The Lancashire Witches*—I used to enjoy in very small print in wretched paper editions procured I know not how; but I had a fervent, secretive way of hiding them under my pillow, and then … while the sleeping dormitory about me faded, dissolved and vanished away … I floated in space with these grotesque and bloodcurdling inventions! (Powys, 125)

The words are typical of those Powys uses when talking about the sadistic literature that formed his vice: lurid books in wretched editions, procured he knows not how. But when we see the iron bar in action, as we do in Cruikshank's memorable illustrations, Jack seems a desperate hero with whom we must identify; violence directed against a prison cannot be counted as sadism.

Harrison Ainsworth (1805–82) is largely a figure of ridicule in subsequent literary history; he went on writing historical novels long after the genre had ceased to be fashionable. Having once been a dandy and a celebrity, he became a shambling, sad recluse whose former friends ignored him. S. M. Ellis suggested, in *William Harrison Ainsworth and his Friends* (1911), that Ainsworth had had an unacknowledged influence over subsequent nineteenth-century novelists; other crtics reckoned the influence, if any, to be deleterious. One, Carl J. Weber, argued for the influence of Ainsworth on Thomas Hardy, concluding:

> But if no one now reads Ainsworth for his own sake, he at least deserves a quiet shelf in a Thomas Hardy library; for as one surveys the Wessex Novels it is clear that the shadow of William Harrison Ainsworth falls across their pages. (Weber, 200)

Subsequent critics seem to have assumed that this shadow must be a bad thing, so that the failings of Hardy's prose style are ascribed to Ainsworth: this is a wretched mark to make in literary history, and a quite unjust one. For Weber recognizes in Ainsworth the source of Hardy's minute and precise description of animal and vegetable life and of natural phenomena. S. M. Ellis had solicited views about Ainsworth from modern writers; Hardy replied, on 4 May 1913: 'I am carried back to the days of my childhood'. (Hardy, 272) Hardy's most

The Castle .
The Red Room .
Door of the Red Room .
George Cruikshank
A door between the Red Room & the Chapel .
The Escape. N.º 1.

explicit debt to Ainsworth is conveyed in *Far From the Madding Crowd* (1874) when Sergeant Troy has the main part in 'Turpin's Ride to York and the Death of Black Bess' in the circus at Greenhill Fair. The fame of Dick Turpin depended on Ainsworth's novel *Rookwood* (1843). Weber points out elsewhere in that novel detailed verbal borrowings from *Rookwood*, arguing that while Ainsworth's influence can be damaging, it is more often transmuted into what is universally recognized as Hardy's genius for natural description: 'Thomas Hardy soon outdistanced his teacher, but it was Ainsworth who taught him how to describe a storm.' (Weber, 196) This augmented lineage will also be important for Powys; though John Cowper proclaimed his enthusiasm for Ainsworth, readers today are likely to overlook Ainsworth in placing Powys in a line that goes back through Hardy to Scott.

Among his contemporaries, Ainsworth had quarrelled with Dickens, and was somewhat cruelly belittled by Thackeray who, in the *Westminster Review* in 1840, remarked of *Jack Sheppard* that 'it seems to us that Mr Cruikshank really created the tale, and that Mr Ainsworth, as it were, only put words to it.' (Weber, 199; see also Meisel, 247; the illustrations on the previous page show the iron bar prominent and ready for use.)

Ainsworth's books have had an insidious reach, a manner of working their way into a wide range of English and foreign literatures, and then, having made their mark, disappearing. In his *Atlas of the European Novel 1800–1900* (1998), Franco Moretti has traced the diffusion of Ainsworth over Europe; we might do the same for England, Scotland, Wales, and Ireland. The escape of Jack Sheppard is one of those remarkable incidents in juvenile or working-class literature, and the place of the iron bar in this set piece is so conspicuous, both in text and illustration, that it is no wonder it lodged in Powys's mind, or should we say, pried open an imagination already stirred by Scott.

The recent publication of Powys's correspondence with Dorothy Richardson brings this rebellious comment, from a late Victorian rather than a belated modernist. In 1937 John Cowper Powys wrote to Dorothy Richardson:

> Heaven help me if I don't hold *Hereward the Wake* and *Westward Ho!* & *John Inglesant* & *the Tower of London* and *Rienzi* and *the Cloister & the Hearth* as of *Immortal Value* compared with the works of Mrs Woolf and Mrs Humphry Ward. (Fouli, 132)

This is not simply a championing of low-brow thrillers, for Powys has just been distinguishing between serious but difficult writers and those who are merely pretentious. The latter are less worth reading than the straightforward historical romances of Harrison Ainsworth. By contrast,

> Top-notch High Brows like Proust & yourself are 'difficult' in the deep Spinozistic sense … of all good & great things (except Charles Dickens & Sir Walter Scott) … .

Exceptionally, Dickens and Scott achieve greatness without involving the reader in difficulties. Powys does not make any such claim of greatness for Ainsworth. Yet in *Jack Sheppard* an iron bar is not just an iron bar, for this one bar serves contrasting ends and purposes. The iron bar that we find in Powys's novels may have been forged by Scott, but it had been wrought anew by Ainsworth—and by Cruikshank.

WORKS CITED

Ainsworth, W. H., *Jack Sheppard: A Romance* (London: Richard Bentley, 1839).

Ellis, Stuart Marsh, *William Harrison Ainsworth and his Friends* (London: John Lane, 1911).

Fouli, Janet, ed.. *The Letters of John Cowper Powys and Dorothy Richardson* (London: Cecil Woolf, 2008).

Hardy, Thomas, *Letters*, ed. R. L. Purdy & M. Millgate, Vol. 4 (Oxford: Clarendon Press, 1984).

Maxwell, Richard, 'A Game of Yes and No: Childhood and Apocalypse in *Porius*', *The Powys Journal* XVI (2006), 84–102.

——, *The Historical Novel in Europe, 1650–1950* (Cambridge University Press, 2009).

Meisel, Martin, *Realizations: Narrative, Pictorial and Theatrical Arts in Nineteenth-Century England* (Princeton UP, 1983).

Moretti, Franco, *Atlas of the European Novel 1800–1900* (London: Verso, 1998).

Powys, John Cowper, *Autobiography* (London: Macdonald, 1967).

Weber, Carl J., 'Ainsworth and Thomas Hardy', *The Review of English Studies*, Vol. 17, No. 66 (April, 1941), 193–200.

REVIEWS

The Letters of John Cowper Powys and Dorothy Richardson

edited by JANET FOULI

London: Cecil Woolf, 2008. 272 pp, ISBN 978-1-897967-27-0 . £35.00.

From the beginning of the correspondence between John Cowper Powys and Dorothy Richardson in 1929, one is aware of the pleasure Powys took in writing to someone whose work he admired. In the first published letter we get a hint of his excitement upon suggesting they meet: 'Apart from my numerous brothers & sisters ... there's no one in England I want to see so much as yourself and it would be rather a sad disappointment to me if fate doesn't allow it.' (16) They would be separated for most of their friendship, first by the Atlantic, and then by the distance between Corwen and London, and would meet only a few times before the early 1950s, when Richardson ceased to write as her health declined. Yet there is a definite bond between them, and the correspondence, instigated by Powys, lasted more than twenty years, from 1929 to 1952. When writing to others, such as Emma Goldman, Powys sometimes had to be buttoned down, but here he enjoys letting himself go, as in this characteristic passage:

> I try & *visualize* the hunched-up, truculant [*sic*], forbidding, impenetrable, pebble-stone-on-the-Chesil-Beach-like Ego into which most of us have the power of transforming ourselves when we 'freeze' at the approach of an enemy ... & starting with this I go ahead with the Self & the Not-Self etc etc etc using all the clap-trap I can recall out of former broodings upon Hegel in order to force my converted ones—of the Third order of Empedocles the Second—into the worship of the Inanimate as the best substitute for 'God', & the place where the wall of the cosmos is *thinnest*, so to speak, & if you put your ear close you can hear the music the *other side*. (68; ellipsis and italics in original)*

Over the course of their correspondence most of Powys's major works come out: *Wolf Solent* appeared just before they met in August 1929. A portion of a letter written in September of that year by Richardson to Peggy Kirkaldy is included: 'The *London Mercury* gives a long article to *Wolf Solent*,

* *An example of JCP's letter writing is shewn on page 6.*

mostly in praise of it. And it seems John has written other books. Dark horse, he never mentioned them.' (17) As it turns out, in the second appendix there is a 1951 letter to the poet and editor Henry Savage in which Richardson expresses what she never mentioned to Powys—her candid opinion about his literary worth:

> [Henry Miller's] adoration of J.C.P.'s work is as mysterious to me as is J.C.P.'s of my own, endlessly reiterated in innumerable letters. For it is not reciprocal. Alan [Alan Odle, Richardson's husband] loved his work and behind him, eagerly reading, I used to hide by quoting A., my own difficulty in getting through anything beyond *Wolf Solent*, bits of *Glastonbury* and *The Pleasures of Literature*, embodying his life-work as lecturer and, for me, his one solid contribution. All the rest I would exchange for Theodore's *Mr. Weston's good wine* [*sic*] and Llewelyn's little book on Switzerland. Miller, I feel, shares J.C.P.'s over-elaboration and reiteration. (247)

This admission can be viewed in any number of ways. Is it a pose created for the benefit of Savage, a relative newcomer in her life? According to George Thomson, editor of *Dorothy Richardson: A Calendar of Letters* (2007), Savage began writing to Richardson in or soon after 1946 'with the purpose, so he claimed, of leading her through argument to assert her outlook and beliefs.'(27) It might be argued that for years Richardson displayed tact, or diplomacy, by not letting her true feelings be known to Powys. For all Powys did to promote her, as the letters show, in lectures and by way of trying to get her collected works published, eagerly reading her work and engaging with it, Dorothy Richardson was unable to offer anything similar in return. She could not match his respect, let alone his enthusiasm, and didn't have the courage or character to say she didn't like this or that work. In a letter to Bernice Elliott, an extract of which is reproduced by Fouli, Richardson refers to *Owen Glendower*: 'Dear John Cowper still inhabits his dark Welsh valley. Things are not, I fear, too easy. He turns out potboilers with amazing rapidity.' (246) When Richardson tells Powys that 'they are right who claim the *Autobiography* as one of the few immortal books of the century' (93), what does she mean, and who is this 'they'? It appears not to include her.

Not only did Powys encourage audiences to read Richardson, he wrote a book on her, news of which brought out from Richardson the gracious comment to Elliott that she was 'not quite sure whether to be jubilant or horrified'. (10) While writers often remember the negative reviews more than the positive ones, generally they do like it when someone goes out of their way to publicize their work. Perhaps, in some other letter to a third party, Richardson expresses gratitude, but the mystery as to why she would be 'jubilant or horrified' about Powys's views is not dispelled.

Literary history has judged Richardson's ranking of Powys's fiction and essays rather differently. John Cowper's literary essays are hard to find, whereas his major fictional works are in many bookstores (new and second-hand), with Faber Finds enabling readers to purchase on-demand novels early and late. However, even now there's no critical consensus about the value of the novels. There is intermittent interest in Dorothy Richardson, as found in the work of Gloria Fromm—above all, her biography of 1977 and her edition of the selected letters, *Windows on Modernism*, in 1995—and, recently, Debora Parsons's assessment of Richardson's role in Modernism's theoretical reflections and formulations: her *Theorists of the Modernist Novel: James Joyce, Dorothy Richardson and Virginia Woolf* was published in 2006. Yet Fouli is close to the mark when she says that both Powys and Richardson are 'now suffering an eclipse; neither writer is really in the canon of English literary studies though both are recognized as significant figures'. (9)

Richardson writes letters that are highly readable, their descriptive passages filled with a poetic attention to detail:

> Here, spring sings aloud & gorse, gently blazing all the winter, flames high now in our midge-haunted tamarisk lane-to-the-sea. But our floods don't abate. I mop gallons from the stone floor of the kitchen, to find them replaced almost before I can turn round. A broad rivulet invades the passage & another the floor of a foolish little bedroom with a no-doubt-heavenly-in-summer outer door, flush with the soil. I cannot, for the rain-din on the roof, hear myself cook, hear, that is to say, whether the stew is just gently whispering or perilously near the boil. (119–20)

The anthropomorphizing of the season, the vegetation, the 'foolish' room, and the natural swerve into domestic affairs, are elements close to Powys's supplications to nature and various spirits, and his comically disastrous encounters with the fire, the stove, and anything to do with maintaining a household. When Richardson writes to give her opinion of *The Pleasures of Literature* over a five-page letter written in February 1939 (155–60) she is at her critical best: attentive to Powys's work, supportive, and engaged with the text, while working out her own opinions.

However, there is a problem with *The Letters of John Cowper Powys and Dorothy Richardson*. The Introduction contains an arguable thesis that the letters 'are not deliberate self-revelations for the public …, for unknown readers were not anticipated by either writer.' (13) This may seem unlikely: all writers must consider the danger that their private writings will enter the public domain. But perhaps Janet Fouli is right, and neither Powys nor Richardson, both of whom had to struggle to get their novels published, ever had an idea that their letters would be printed. More seriously, for any editor of correspondence involving John Cowper, to write, as Fouli does, that one particular exchange of letters forms a 'self-portrait projecting each of them in his preoccupations and his environment, and also a mirror, showing how each of them sees the other' (13), is to say only that at heart this volume is indistinct from other volumes of Powys letters. This actually underplays the particular interest of this volume.

Further, when we look at the editor's bold announcement that this correspondence 'show[s] how each of them sees the other', and then at the letter to Savage where Richardson reveals her honest opinion about Powys's work, we see something very far from truthful 'showing'. There is a touch of impatience behind Richardson's complaint over Powys's admiration of her novels 'endlessly reiterated in innumerable letters', as if she felt put upon by a tiresome fan. Fouli provides the material to arrive at this conclusion, and it's disconcerting that she doesn't notice the contradiction in her claim. We are left to wonder what else Richardson thought about Powys and his work which went unstated to him but which she was clear about to others, or kept to herself. The editorial apparatus is of little help here.

Indeed, the Notes, which occupy the back of the book, fail to provide enough context. A few examples will illustrate this. Powys mentions a book titled *Quiet Interiors* (43), for which the note gives little beyond its author's name, E. B. C. Jones. It is surely worth mentioning that the book was highly praised by Katherine Mansfield. The planet Eros that he refers to (44) goes without a note, though a Google search calls up much about it. When Powys notes that Richardson 'became a Bugloss' (81) the meaning is mysterious. This appears to be a noxious plant, but is there some other meaning it might have? Might it also be the name of a character from some literary work? Further on, a Dr Bertrand Allinson and a medication named Yadil are referred to, but no note accompanies these references (90–92), though a Google search reveals that Allinson was an advocate of vegetarianism. French goes untranslated (98); when Richardson asks 'Is the passing of Mary Butts a blow for you? For us it is' (121), readers are sent, and not right away, to a note that tells of a publication by this still little-known writer. The same fate is imposed on 'Shaw, Webb & Wells' (204), where Shaw and Wells are clear from the context, but anyone not familiar with Webb will find no more about him except that his first name was Sidney, and that is to be learnt only in the Index.

From 30 March 1930 to 29 September 1932 there are only two letters from Richardson. More information on her life, in addition to the extracts from Powys's diaries, would have been useful here. There are many places where a reader would be thankful for entries identifying Peggy Kirkaldy, Henry Savage or Bernice Elliott. It would also have been good to have more than one paragraph on Richardson's last years. In general Fouli has not taken the opportunity to fill in the biographical context, or address particular biographical issues, in adequate detail. She does, however, decipher Powys's notoriously bad handwriting and his erratic placement of words on a page, which is no small achievement, and for which she deserves appropriate commendation.

At a time when people are purchasing Kindles, or not purchasing books at all, making books harder to read, through the use of endnotes, is perverse and self-defeating. In the case of *The Letters of John Cowper Powys and Dorothy Richardson*, the material placed at the back of the book could have been turned into footnotes. Why any publisher—and I'm not singling out Cecil Woolf with this complaint—should make a reader flick two hundred or so pages ahead of where he or she is has always been mysterious; whatever the reason, the effect is discourteous. Other readers will of course object to footnotes: they clog the page, look unseemly, disrupt the illusion that one is reading inside a sealed world, or prevent a smooth reading process. Yet endnotes are far more disruptive than footnotes. In a collection of letters such as this, footnotes would not have taken up much space.

Despite these reservations, *The Letters of John Cowper Powys and Dorothy Richardson* is an enjoyable collection, filled with wonderfully unpredictable thoughts, and two distinct modes of writing. It would be fitting to close with an example of each writer's style. After a meeting between Powys and Richardson, and Phyllis Playter and Alan Odle, in 1934, Powys writes: 'After being with you two I felt a glow that lifted me on a wave of foamless content with the possibilities of existence & I didn't care what I'd blurted out or what blunderings I'd committed; and I knew you'd take Phyllis just right and as she likes to be taken, as your words now prove—not as if she were [a] pilgrim swallowed by Gargantua with his lettuce, but like a a [*sic*] girl with her own thoughts as she rides on the Centaur's back!' (85) Richardson's letters provide views into her own marriage: 'For five days we've been here, drunk with release, both of us, for Alan at home is dishwasher & boot-cleaner, breakfast-getter & toast-for-tea maker, from every kind of chore; drunk also with the excitements of urban centrality, keeping us, who are flush with the roadway, with half an eye permanently slewed round to see who is passing, & both ears wide for farm-yard sounds & meadow-sounds & the occasional thundering of the omnibus down the lane.' (122–6) Whatever the writers' wishes or expectations, the editor, and the publisher especially, deserve our thanks for making these letters available. Though the readership may be wider than the letter-writers intended, it is likely to find much to appreciate and admire.

Jeff Bursey

The Letters of John Cowper Powys and Emma Goldman

edited by DAVID GOODWAY

London: Cecil Woolf, 2008. 188pp, ISBN *978-1-897967-84-3. £30.00*

This volume consists of the 58 extant letters exchanged by John Cowper Powys and Emma Goldman in the brief period 1936–40. They thus cover a most crucial time in the history of Anarchism, the years of the Spanish Civil War when Anarchism seemed closer than ever before (or since) to whatever might take the place of 'political power' should such be exercised by Anarchists. Emma Goldman's letters remind us of how devastating was their failure, and thus of the strength of the belief, held until November 1938, that the Spanish Anarchists might have prevailed.

Powys as a correspondent can often be blandly intimate; this is a disconcerting and paradoxical effect achieved by a highly formalized rhetoric of disclosure on his part, together with a presumed intimacy with his correspondent's character and mind. He engages in plenty of this in these letters to Emma Goldman, even allowing himself in a letter of 9 January 1937 to commit an acronym in an affectation of familiarity:

> I have been so grateful for the propaganda-information sent me (in English) from Barcelona & have sent it on to sympathetic friends. And now comes this most exciting letter about your being the actual accredited representative here of both the C.N.T. & the F.A.I.!

The editor, David Goodway, spells out all the acronyms and supplies the necessary political and historical background; and he assumes throughout John Cowper's whole-hearted support for the Anarchist cause. The sheer tonal oddity of these letters tends to escape comment. The chief interest of this volume may lie in its situating of John Cowper Powys in relation to the Spanish Civil War, and in shedding further light on the most celebrated anarchist of the age. There is another source of interest, however, which should attract those who are amused by the games that Powys plays as a letter-writer. Here his interest is to keep Goldman's respect and friendship while making what to some readers may appear to be a minimal effort to understand her politics.

By June 1938 Emma had seen through his game, which he thereafter intensified with a degree of flattery that prompted her twice to write that, had he been Irish, she'd think he'd kissed the Blarney Stone. Powys's flattery is accompanied by confession, that proclaimed candour that appears to make vulnerable the one confessing, but actually disarms the one addressed. On 15 June 1938 John Cowper expressed the hope that Emma Goldman would have her dreams realized in Spain. Two months later, during the decisive Battle of the Ebro, Emma replied (16 August 1938) by quoting back at him a long sentence from his letter, in order to comment:

> You will forgive me, I know, for saying that there is a contradiction in this very first paragraph. It is wherein you speak of a 'country really free' and yet seem to think that government is necessary to maintain this ideal. ... Another mistake you are making, dear friend, is in your belief in the need of 'centralized authority'. This is precisely what the Spanish Anarchists do *not* want .... I am taking the liberty of sending you a copy of 'Anarcho-Syndicalism—Theory and Practice' .... .

Having had his assumptions corrected and having been sent some reading matter, John Cowper replied within just two days, on 18 August 1938:

> I am so grateful to you for this book on Anarcho-Syndicalism. ... Yes the frank truth is, old friend, I am simply ignorant .... And I think many many well-meaning bourgeois people are as ignorant as I am. None of us *can* remain ignorant of the ideas of Communism for we all have some young friends in our circle ready to din into our ears the Moscow arguments and propaganda. ... But you must remember, dear Emma Goldman, that you yourself are the only anarchist I know or have ever known save a very gentle ... printer in Boston ...; and I have never read *one single anarchistic book or life or even pamphlet!*

That they liked each other is clear: John Cowper told others how proud he was to have such a famous friend, just as Emma Goldman expressed to others her appreciation of what John Cowper's support had meant to her during these difficult years that she spent in England. They were keen to overlook differences, as when (on 13 December 1938) Emma responds to John Cowper's confession: 'I appreciate your frankness in admitting that you have never read anything about Anarchism, but I really do not believe you. …'

Their friendship, and loyalty, had its roots some twenty years back when they had met in radical circles in New York. One of the treasures in this volume is the reprinting of a report in *Mother Earth* (May 1916) of 'The Free Speech and Birth Control Dinner' held at the Brevoort Hotel, at which both Emma Goldman and Powys spoke. After talking about Milton as a libertarian, 'Mr Powys said that he was appalled by the depth of his own ignorance in relation to the subject of birth control, but, in a general way, he wished to be counted as one in sympathy with the birth control movement and with its champion Emma Goldman.' The item is not recorded in the bibliographies of either Langridge or Thomas. More surprisingly, Emma Goldman's own account of the evening, in *Living My Life* (1931), where Powys figures prominently, has also been overlooked; the relevant pages are reprinted here.

Their mutual friends in those days included Theodore Dreiser, Colonel Charles Erskine Scott Wood and Maurice Browne of the Chicago Little Theatre. Also valuable in these letters are the sidelights they throw on the New York in which Emma and John Cowper had once known each other, both distantly and prominently. When Emma writes to John Cowper for the first time, on 1 January 1936, it is because she has been given his address by Maurice Browne. It is likely that Emma had renewed her contact with Browne through 'my old dear friend, Paul Robeson' (28 March 1938). He and Emma had been friends since 1926, and she would feel dreadfully betrayed when Robeson abandoned his ties with Anarchism on turning to Communism in 1938. Paul Robeson had been discovered as an actor in 1929, when Maurice Browne had watched *Show Boat* and decided that Robeson should play Othello, as he did in 1930, with Peggy Ashcroft as Desdemona. Maurice Browne, the producer, took the part of Iago. Thus we find John Cowper just a step away from one of the legendary theatrical productions of the twentieth century.

Whether one's interests lie in Anarchism and the Spanish Civil War, or in Powys and his circle, this correspondence confirms that John Cowper was far from isolated, and was hardly neglected. Though by then living in Corwen, Powys could not be forgotten for he had been thoroughly immersed in some of the most powerful currents of twentieth-century culture. Through his editorial work David Goodway has opened up a range of John Cowper's contacts and connections, many of them hitherto little investigated.

Charles Lock

NOTES ON CONTRIBUTORS

MELVON L. ANKENY is an emeritus faculty librarian of The Ohio State University Libraries now living in Missoula, Montana, USA.

LOUISE DE BRUIN lives in Mappowder. She joined the Powys Society in 1976 and has been—in various roles—an active member since 1989. Her edition of Mary Casey's journal, *A Net in Water*, was published in 1994. In recent years she has been co-organiser of the Society's Annual Conference.

JEFF BURSEY first became interested in Powys when writing a Master's thesis on Henry Miller. He now writes for journals in Canada, the UK and the US. His first book, *Verbatim: A Novel*, told in lists, letters and dual-column political debates, will be published by Enfield & Wizenty in the fall of 2010.

JANET FOULI is a retired lecturer in English literature and lives in Tunis. Her thesis, *Structure and Identity: the Creative Imagination in Dorothy Richardson's* Pilgrimage was published in 1995 by the Publications de la Faculté des Lettres à Manouba in Tunis. She is the editor of *The Letters of John Cowper Powys and Dorothy Richardson* (London: Cecil Woolf, 2008).

FLORENCE MARIE-LAVERROU is a senior lecturer at the University de Pau et les Pays de l'Adour (France). She defended her thesis on J. C. Powys in December 2003 and since then she has published several articles on his Wessex novels.

CHARLES LOCK is Professor of English Literature at the University of Copenhagen and acting editor of *The Powys Journal*. Recent publications include essays on the contemporary poets Geoffrey Hill, Roy Fisher and Anne Blonstein.

RICHARD MAXWELL teaches in the Comparative Literature Department at Yale University and is the editor of *The Powys Journal*. His monograph, *The Historical Novel in Europe*, published by Cambridge University Press in 2009, includes discussions of *Owen Glendower* and *Porius*.

ELAINE MENCHER, initially trained as a teacher, lived, and studied music, in France. She has given recitals of J. S. Bach's keyboard music at London venues such as the Wigmore Hall, Purcell Room, Leighton House and St Martin-in-the-Fields. Her passion for literature and the writing of T. F. Powys led to the establishment of the Brynmill Press T. F. Powys Series, which she has helped to research and edit, her latest work in that series being the independently edited *Selected Early Works* (2003).

ANGELIKA REICHMANN graduated from Debrecen University (Hungary) in 1998 and gained her doctorate in 2006 in the Comparative Literary Studies Program of the same university. She has been publishing articles on Dostoevsky, Andrey Bely and John Cowper Powys since 1997. Her most recent works include analyses of Dostoevsky's *Devils* and Powys's *Wolf Solent* and *Weymouth Sands* from a psychoanalytic perspective, focusing on the phenomena of narcissism and the abject.